STRATEGIC
QUESTIONING

STRATEGIC QUESTIONING

Ronald T. Hyman

Rutgers University

PRENTICE-HALL, INC. Englewood Cliffs, New Jersey 07632

Library of Congress Cataloging in Publication Data

HYMAN, RONALD T
    Strategic questioning.

    Includes bibliographical references and index.
    1. Questioning.   I. Title.
LB1027.H94   371.3'7   79-783
ISBN   0-13-851055-5

© 1979 by Ronald T. Hyman

Printed in the United States of America
10 9 8 7 6 5 4 3 2 1

Prentice-Hall International, Inc., *London*
Prentice-Hall of Australia Pty. Limited, *Sydney*
Prentice-Hall of Canada, Ltd., *Toronto*
Prentice-Hall of India Private Limited, *New Delhi*
Prentice-Hall of Japan, Inc., *Tokyo*
Prentice-Hall of Southeast Asia Pte. Ltd., *Singapore*
Whitehall Books Limited, *Wellington, New Zealand*

IT IS BETTER TO ASK SOME
OF THE QUESTIONS
THAN TO KNOW ALL THE ANSWERS.

James Thurber

CONTENTS

SIX: Twenty-five Questioning Dialogues: A Manual of Questioning Techniques **97**

Introduction

The aim of this book is to help you become an effective, strategic questioner. I, like every other teacher, ask questions, and I have pursued the matter of classroom questioning for a number of years as part of my continued interest in the verbal interaction between teachers and students. Based on my knowledge of the research on questioning and the classroom behavior of teachers I have sought to improve my own ability to ask questions when teaching. The key to my efforts to improve lies in the concept of strategic questioning.

Teachers need a strategy for asking questions simply because with a strategy they have a framework within which to determine the questions they will ask. The strategy serves as a guide and helps to answer questions they raise about what action they can and should take with students. A guide is necessary in planning for teaching but even more so while in the actual act of teaching. The interaction between teacher and student is so complex and generally so rapid as to prevent long deliberations. Even with careful and comprehensive planning no teacher can—or should—know ahead of time exactly which questions to ask at a given moment. Every teacher constantly monitors the ongoing situation in order to tailor the interaction to the demands of the situation. Therefore, the ability at a given juncture in the lesson to ask an appropriate question, one which will continue the forward thrust of the interaction, requires a framework.

This framework provided by a questioning strategy reduces the strain on the teacher and offers a sense of security so that he or she feels that all will not be lost when the unexpected occurs. Thus, strategy promotes confidence and ease which in turn communicate a positive tone to the students.

A strategy also provides a cumulative effect. Individual questions spur students to think. When the questions follow a particular sequence there is definite hidden impact. Single questions which are appropriate are needed, but the overall impact on the interaction stems from the strategy of questioning which combines the individual questions into a cohesive whole. From her research on teacher behavior Hilda Taba realized this point, and it led her to develop her work on strategies of teaching. "The impact of teaching lies not alone in its single acts but in the manner in which these acts are combined into a pattern."[1]

The concept of strategy and the use of strategy are ancient and have been with us in teaching for centuries. In reply to Meno's request to teach him, Socrates sets up a demonstration. In this demonstration Socrates interrupts himself after each crucial step in his strategy in order to comment on what has happened so that Meno will not miss the importance of each step. Furthermore, during the interruption Socrates introduces the next step in the demonstration so as to guide Meno in observing Socrates, the master strategist.[2]

Socrates understands what his strategy is, knows its various parts, and has a keen insight about teaching it to others. Hence, he proceeds one "step" at a time in his demonstration and points out the essence of his "step by step" procedure before and after each step. By this demonstration for Meno, Socrates shows his mastery of teaching on two levels, teaching and teaching how to teach.

Indeed, the very word "strategy" is derived from the Greek word for "general." A Greek *strategos* devised a careful plan so as to lead his men successfully in achieving their goals in battle. In time, the word "strategy" came to apply generically to endeavors where a

---

[1] Hilda Taba, Samuel Levine, Freeman F. Elzey, *Thinking in Elementary School Children* (San Francisco: San Francisco State College, 1964), p. 55.

[2] See the chapter on the Socratic Method in Ronald T. Hyman, *Ways of Teaching*, 2nd ed. (Philadelphia: J.B. Lippincott Company, 1974).

leader uses a plan involving a series of steps. So as to have an explicit referent for the word "strategy" as it applies to teaching, I will use the following definition: *Strategy is a carefully prepared plan involving a sequence of steps designed to achieve a given goal.*

As I developed various questioning strategies appropriate for different situations in teaching, I began to teach them to college students in class and to other people in in-service workshops. The reception was most positive. What came to light was the previously *unexpressed* need teachers felt about learning to improve their questioning—unexpressed because most people were uneasy in admitting that they needed help in so basic a teaching skill. I then also developed a series of questioning dialogues as a method for training people to learn and practice techniques, or tactics, to use along with other strategies. The response to these questioning dialogues by every type of person involved was especially favorable.

In this way this book on strategic questioning is an outgrowth of many years as a researcher, teacher, and questioner. The intent of this book is to provide you a usable text on questioning which goes beyond merely learning to categorize questions you prepare ahead of time or ask as the situation evolves. Also, the focus is on teacher questioning without much mention of student questioning so you can concentrate on your own classroom behavior, which is the easiest way for you to alter classroom interaction.

This focus on teacher questioning does not claim that questioning is the only thing teachers do. Though teacher questions are central and essential to teaching, they are not necessarily the most important behavior in any given teaching situation. Teachers do perform other critical acts as well. We ought not to lose sight of this for then we might forget the larger context of teaching. The focus of this book is my response to the call of the London Association for the Teaching of English, "to improve our procedures in school in such a way that language becomes a facilitating force in learning rather than a barrier bristling with formidable difficulties."[3]

Chapter 1 presents a brief comment on the purposes of teacher questions in order to set the tone and a context for the remaining chapters. Chapter 2 offers a set of criteria and a set of cognitive categories for understanding the types of questions teachers ask.

[3]Harold Rosen, "A Language Policy across the Curriculum," in *Language, the Learner, and the School*, rev. ed. (Harmondsworth, England: Penguin Books, Ltd., 1971) pg. 160.

Chapter 3 deals with other considerations such as recall and the yes/no form, which cut across all the cognitive categories. The purpose of these chapters is to sensitize you to the various types of questions teachers ask. Use of the categories will provide a way of analyzing questions as one key step in the improvement process.

Chapters 4 and 5 concern themselves with strategies. Chapter 4 offers five general strategies, that is, overarching ways of organizing your questions. It offers the concepts of peaks and plateaus and explains the familiar concepts of inductive and deductive questioning. Chapter 5 offers fifteen specific strategies devoted to such cognitive tasks as generalizing, explaining, and analyzing values. These strategies include the questions asked by you as the teacher and the cognitive tasks performed by the respondents. The purpose of these two chapters is to make available to you foundations to build on as you work on your own improvement. These chapters are not analytical ones but rather tools for implementation which you can modify to fit your individual need.

Chapter 6 is a training manual consisting of twenty-five questioning dialogues. These dialogues offer you a method for learning and practicing various tactics which will aid you in strategic questioning. This chapter, too, is not an analytical one. If you wish, you can use the questioning dialogues to create your own workshop experience. All you need is two other adventurous and dedicated people.

You will note that Chapter 6 offers probing tactics which do not necessarily appear in the fifteen specific strategies. The reason is two-fold. The responses you receive from your questions may deserve further attention due to their uniqueness. Second, you may wish to embellish the prepared strategy you are using from Chapter 5. Thus, you will use these probing tactics when you see fit in the fifteen specific strategies.

Chapter 7 treats the larger teaching context of your questioning and sets forth the interrelationship between strategies and goals. This chapter offers three types of teaching strategies and two types of goals. It also shows how questioning is important to each type of teaching strategy and goal.

Chapter 8 is the concluding chapter which summarizes key points of the book and offers some final points on questioning. It shows the importance of student questioning and therefore the need for teachers to teach their students how to ask questions.

Chapters 2, 3, 4, and 5 include nine practice exercises. I believe that these exercises will help you master the ideas you read about and further your internalization of them by involving you actively with the material. I urge you not to skip these exercises for I have found them to be an effective device for learning about questioning. For the first few exercises I offer my own responses as a guide. For the last few I leave you completely on your own as my way of saying that I believe that by then you will be independently on track.

All in all, I have designed and written this book to be one which you can and will use to learn about questions and to improve your questioning as a teacher.

STRATEGIC
QUESTIONING

ONE

THE PURPOSE
OF TEACHER QUESTIONS

Teachers have always asked questions and they always will. They do so because asking questions is essential to teaching. Just as it is impossible to conceive of classroom teaching without talking between teacher and student, it is impossible to conceive of teaching without asking questions.

It is natural for you as a teacher to ask questions, because questions serve many purposes. When you ask a question, you may achieve several purposes simultaneously. No matter how many purposes you accomplish, however, your question serves mainly to cause someone to think along a particular line. A question serves a double purpose by its very nature: *It prods the respondent to think* so as to supply a response, and it directs that respondent to think *about a particular topic*.

Let us consider this dual purpose by using a hypothetical situation. Suppose you ask a student, Jonathan Johnson, this question: "What effect did the severe cold wave of 1977 have on the United States?" Unless the student has before him a list already prepared from which he can read to you, your question spurs him to think about the cold wave. Your question specifically solicits from him an effect of the cold wave rather than a cause of it, his opinion of it, or information about its length and intensity.

The student may respond, "It caused the government meteorological department to try to discover why the cold air coming down from Canada didn't get warmed up by the warm air coming over from the west coast." This response may surprise you somewhat. You may have expected a response dealing with the subsequent shortage of natural gas for homes and factories in the Midwest and Eastern U.S. Nevertheless, you must accept his reply as appropriate; you have prodded him to offer an effect of the cold wave and he has done so.

If you wish to probe this student's response, you certainly may do so by asking other questions, by permitting someone else to ask a question, or by reacting either to him or to his remarks yourself. You may wish to accept his response and then elicit other effects of the cold wave from other students. Whatever your decision, the question has achieved its primary purpose. You have gotten the student to perform the cognitive task that you asked him to perform. Research shows that students manifest the thinking teachers request of them.[1]

A question, as noted above, may serve several purposes simultaneously. In addition to the purpose of spurring the student to think about the cold wave, it is certainly possible for you to have other purposes or motives in asking him to respond. You may have questioned him in order to:

a. get him, in particular, to participate in the class. (Perhaps he is a new student and this will get him involved with the class.)
b. find out what he knows about the 1977 cold wave. (You'd like to learn what he knows.)
c. get a discussion on the cold wave going. (You know that Jonathan has novel ideas about its effect.)

---

[1] Arno Bellack, Herbert M. Kliebard, Ronald T. Hyman, and Frank L. Smith, Jr., *The Language of the Classroom* (New York: Teachers College Press, 1966), p. 125 and John H. Lake, "The Influence of Wait-Time on the Verbal Dimension of Student Inquiry Behavior" (Doctoral dissertation, Rutgers University, 1973).

d. attract his attention. (He's been busily talking with his neighbor across the aisle, disturbing the class, and he is lost to the ongoing discussion.)

e. provide a springboard for you to talk about the cold wave of 1977 since you're so concerned about it yourself. (You've long been concerned about the energy crisis and you want to explore the issues raised by the cold wave and its effect.)

f. give Jonathan a chance to shine before his classmates. (Jonathan's in need of some positive peer recognition in light of his near disastrous performance in small group discussion on the Carter-Ford race of November, 1976.)

g. test his learning of the material in the booklet about energy. (He's doing some independent work and you want to test him to see if he can list at least four effects of the cold wave as given in the booklet. By testing him you'll find out how well he's learning by himself.)

h. initiate a lesson on cause and effect relationships. (You've been heading toward the exploration of logical thinking and relationships between events. This will be an excellent vehicle for involving the students in this topic because they know about the cold wave from their personal lives.)

i. review what you talked about in a small group during your free period near the end of school yesterday. (The discussion you had was so invigorating that the small group thought you should raise the topic with the entire class. This question will serve to bring out a summary of the points raised in that small group so as to let everyone know what you talked about there.)

j. determine to what extent Jonathan can do "think it out by yourself" thinking. (He's got lots of data before him from your previous class discussions. You'd like to see how well he can take those facts and integrate them into something new.)

This list of ten purposes concerns the question you asked of Jonathan in regard to the cold wave of 1977. Other questions may have additional purposes. For example, you can ask a question in order to:

k. stimulate the creative thinking of Jonathan.

l. request Jonathan to offer a value judgment and its justification on a given issue, such as the energy crisis.

m.   determine the cause(s) of a given event, such as the cold wave of 1977 or London's drought in 1976.
n.   solve a perplexing problem, such as how to insulate an exterior house wall.
o.   state some facts about an event, such as the temperature high, low, and average during the cold wave.

In short, there are many purposes which a teacher can achieve by asking a question. One question may serve two or more purposes at the same time. You yourself may not be entirely sure of all your purposes. You may not even realize what the main result of asking a particular question will be until you look back on the response you received. (It occurs even more often that the respondent doesn't realize the purpose or purposes of your question. The respondent is too busy coping with the primary dual purpose of your question to be able to figure out other purposes.)

In the list above some fifteen purposes for questions appear. The listing of these purposes in no way implies approval, but it does indicate that such purposes do exist. One purpose in particular deserves specific mention in this regard. To ask a question as a disciplinary measure subverts the primary purpose of making a person think about a given topic. The teacher who uses questioning as a technique for maintaining order, saying in effect, "If you don't behave properly or pay attention, I'll attack you with a question which may well embarrass you before your classmates," does not foster a classroom atmosphere supportive of thinking. The students would be too concerned about threats and intimidation to put their brains to critical and creative work. Moreover, the teacher is acting in a duplicitous manner by pretending to be concerned with thinking while actually being concerned with control. Rather than being subversive and duplicitous, the teacher would be better off calling for the students' attention in a straightforward way.

You must also be careful that you don't play the "guess what's in my mind" game when you question a student. It is pointless to continue asking students the same question until they respond with the answer you had in mind all along. First, this guessing game tells students that rather than have them think, you want them to give you what you want to hear. Second, you imply that you value your thinking but not theirs. If the question does have a correct answer which is necessary for moving ahead with your strategy (e.g., How much is two times five?), then you must consider modifying your approach. You can shift the question or follow another option suggested in questioning dialogue 23 (chapter 6). In short, the guessing game, by creating an expectation that steers the students away from thought, undermines your efforts to encourage students to think.

Exploring the purposes of teachers' questions may give you a clue as to why questions are essential to teaching. You might be able to accomplish most, if not all, of these purposes through some other pedagogical approach. It is easier and more sensible, however, to ask questions to achieve these purposes, since questions are a direct approach. Why try to avoid a direct approach in favor of a less direct one? Moreover, since you achieve similar purposes in your everyday life by asking questions, it is only natural to ask questions when you teach.

No other single pedagogical technique yields so much return for your effort. Just as it would be impossible to have the use of your two arms without ever utilizing them, it is impossible for you to have the ability to ask questions and never do so. Can you imagine leading a discussion with students and not asking a question? Can you imagine conducting a review session without asking a question?

TWO

QUESTION TYPES: COGNITIVE PROCESSES

When we look at questions as central elements within teaching strategies, as a means of achieving teaching goals, and as a key part of the language game of teaching, we must formulate a set of categories to classify questions. A set of categories for questions is helpful in that it allows us to see commonalities, differences, and patterns among specific items. In our lives we categorize and apply categories constantly as a means of coping with the thousands of details we deal with daily. Witness the common nouns in our language—chairs, shoes, cars, trees, books—which establish categories of objects. It would be impossible to communicate with other people if we didn't have or couldn't use categories.

In this chapter I shall briefly treat the criteria needed for meaningful categorizing and then present a set of cognitive categories that has proven useful.

CRITERIA FOR A SET OF CATEGORIES

The prime requisite for a set of question categories is that the categories relate closely to the purposes of questions. A category system based on the length of the question or based on the number of words needed to answer the question would be pointless, if not misleading. When we review the research literature on questioning, we find several systems that classify questions according to the cognitive (thinking) process which the questions require the respondent to perform.

The four best known of such systems derive from the work of (1) Aschner and her associates, who built directly on Guilford's theory of the intellect; (2) Bellack and his associates; (3) Bloom and his associates; and (4) Taba and her associates.[1] Though there are overlaps in the categories established by these four systems, each is distinctive because each views thinking from a different perspective.

Aschner, basing her system on Guilford's psychological framework, uses productive thinking as her perspective. Bellack, basing his system primarily on the work of the British logicians studying the relationship between language and thought, uses verification processes as his perspective. Bloom, interested in establishing a way of classifying test questions aimed at measuring achievement of cognitive educational objectives, developed his popular taxonomy of cognitive objectives. (Despite its popularity, Bloom's work is seriously flawed. Bloom, in his later book on the affective domain, states that it is not known whether his cognitive "taxonomy" is actually a hierarchical ordering of cognitive objectives or only a simple categorizing of cognitive processes with no rank ordering at all. Though the title of the system claims a taxonomy and most users of the system act on the basis that it is taxonomy, no hierarchical order among the categories has been demonstrated. Bloom himself acknowledges this.[2] Hence, any talk of "higher order," "lower order," and cognitive "levels of questions" based on Bloom's work is inappropriate

---

[1]Ronald T. Hyman, ed., *Teaching: Vantage Points for Study* (Philadelphia: J. B. Lippincott Co., 1974), Ch. 12, 13, 15, 38.
[2]David R. Krathwohl, Benjamin S. Bloom, and Bertram B. Masia, *Taxonomy of Educational Objectives: Handbook II: Affective Domain* (New York: David McKay Company, 1964), p. 12.

and misleading even though many people would like to be able to use such terms as congenial to their educational ideas.) Taba, influenced by the psychological work of Piaget and other psychologists concerned with cognitive maturation, designed her system of categories using the perspective of cognitive function within teaching.

Another essential requisite for a set of question categories is that the categories be reliable and easy to use. If we have questions before us, we should find it easy to classify them into the various categories. What is more, other people should be able to classify the questions similarly. If we look at the categories themselves, then we should find it easy to make up questions to fit each of the categories. Not all category systems are reliable and easy to use in this sense. The classifying of questions according to different systems becomes so difficult and open to individual interpretation that a question which is Type X for one person turns out to be Type Y for someone else. This is why a category system may appear simple and reliable on paper, when in practice it turns out to be complicated and not as useful as claimed.

Finally, a set of categories has to be compatible with the user. The user has to feel comfortable using the categories and must feel that they make sense. The user must not feel forced by the categories, but must feel comfortable with a good fit that facilitates the task at hand. The user must feel that the categories help rather than hinder a discussion about questions.

Keeping these facts in mind, the following cognitive categories and comments are offered. We have used them in classes, in workshops, and in research. We hope that you, too, will find them useful and helpful.

COGNITIVE PROCESSES

There are four main types of cognitive process questions but only the first three appear in most classrooms with any degree of regularity. The four main types are:

1. Definitional
2. Empirical
3. Evaluative
4. Metaphysical

This method of categorizing questions follows the system that was used by researchers[3] and described by John Wilson.[4]

Three essential points about the categories must be kept in mind. First, since a questioner expects to elicit a response, we classify a question in terms of the response it should elicit. Second, we view the response as a statement which asserts that something is true. The response makes a truth claim. We classify the question and its response, therefore, according to the way we would verify the truth of the response. Third, there is no hierarchy intended or implied with these categories. Definitional thinking is not a lower order of thinking than Empirical thinking. Empirical is not lower than Evaluative. Within the subparts of each type there is also no hierarchy. There is, however, a matter of complexity. Obviously it is more complex to give an opinion supported by reasons than to give only an opinion. It is more complex to state the causes of an event and thus explain it than to state only a fact about the event.

Let us explore each of the four main types, giving specific examples to clarify their meaning.

Definitional.

Questions in this category ask you to define a word, term, or phrase. In responding to a definitional question you give descriptive characteristics, or a label, or a specific instance of the word as you give its meaning. For example,

a. What is air pressure?

[3]Arno A. Bellack, Herbert M. Kliebard, Ronald T. Hyman, and Frank L. Smith, Jr., *The Language of the Classroom* (New York: Teachers College Press, 1966).
[4]John Wilson, *Language and the Pursuit of Truth* (Cambridge: Cambridge University Press, 1953).

b. Give me an example of a percussion instrument so I'll know what it means.
c. What does it mean to "sell short" in the stock market?
d. What do you call an object that children play with to have fun?

These questions are all categorized as definitional in that we verify the truth of their response statements by referring to the various sets of rules about language we have established. You know that "hot" is the opposite of "cold," for example, because in our language we have all agreed to use the words in this way. You do not go to the world of your sense perceptions for evidence about the truth of a definition. You do not go to an almanac to find out what "hot" means but rather to a dictionary which reports how people use the word in communication. "Hot" means what it does according to the dictionary only because we who speak English have agreed on a meaning for that word. We can alter definitions and add new words to our language by agreeing to the changes.

Empirical.

Questions in this category ask you to give responses based on your sense perceptions of the world. They ask for facts, comparisons and contrasts among facts, explanations of events, conclusions based on facts, or inferences which go beyond the facts on hand. For example,

A. Specific Facts
  a. Who wrote *Lord of the Flies*, Steinbeck or Golding?
  b. When was the Israeli surprise raid at Entebbe?
  c. Will it rain next Tuesday?
  d. What will New York City look like in 2099?
B. General Facts, Conclusions, or Inferences Based on Facts
  a. What generalization can you make now about all the Presidents from Eisenhower to Carter?
  b. What conclusion do you draw from the fact that there is a health warning on every pack of cigarettes?
  c. What do you infer from the fact that sparrows don't fly south in the winter?

C. Comparisons and Contrasts
  a. What's the difference between skim milk, whole milk, and dry milk?
  b. In what ways is chess like backgammon? How is it different?
D. Explanations of Events or States of Affairs
  a. Why did the state trooper stop your car on the turnpike? (Give the *cause* of a specific event.)
  b. If you rush the net after you serve the ball, what might happen to you? (Give the *consequence* of an event.)
  c. How do you play the game hide and seek? (Tell the *sequence* of procedures or events.)
  d. What causes paint to dry up so fast? (Give *causes* of a general event.)
  e. Would there have been a Watergate investigation if McGovern rather than Nixon would have won the election of 1972?

These questions are all categorized as empirical in that we verify the truth of their responses by referring to our sense perceptions. The responses to these questions state that something is the case. We verify the assertions made by observing with our senses and then deciding whether or not the statement is true. We do not go to a dictionary to verify a claim that John Steinbeck wrote *Lord of the Flies*. We check the book cover or the library card index to find out that William Golding is the author. Similarly, we find out what might happen if we rush the net by observing ourselves or by speaking with someone else who observes that event.

The question "Will it rain next Tuesday?" and other questions dealing with the future are also empirical even though we cannot verify the responses immediately. At the appropriate time, though, we can verify the claim that "It will rain on Tuesday." On Tuesday we observe the weather to find out if it is raining. So too with the question "Would there have been a Watergate investigation if McGovern rather than Nixon had won the election of 1972?" Though we cannot ever verify responses to this question because they are based on *contrary-to-fact conditions* (we can never *know* what events would have taken place in the past if things were different), we classify this question as an empirical one. (Our line of thought follows the "if/then" pattern, the same pattern used in response to other questions dealing with actual events, such as "If you open the refrigerator, what will happen?") The question about Watergate and McGovern is a contrary-to-fact question, a main type of "divergent" question.[5] It calls for a creative response since the respondent must draw on known information and create a fresh statement which cannot be assessed as right or wrong. It allows and encourages the respondent to use imagination in the creation of a response to what might have been.

Evaluative.

Questions in this category ask you to give responses that state your own personal value judgments. Value judgments praise, blame, commend, criticize, or rate something. They deal with attitudes, feelings, morals, personal beliefs, and policies. Questions which request you to state or interpret someone else's empirical statements or value judgments are not categorized as evaluative because you do not give your own personal value judgment. Examples of evaluative questions include

A Opinion
  a. Who is your favorite twentieth century American novelist?
  b. Do you believe we ought to lower the voting age to 16?
  c. Was Lyndon Johnson an excellent, average, or poor President?
  d. If you were President Kennedy, would *you* have invaded the Bay of Pigs?
B. Justifications of Opinions
  a. What are your reasons for saying that *Hamlet* is the greatest tragedy ever written?
  b. Why do you believe in legalizing pot?

---

[5]James J. Gallagher and Mary Jane Aschner, "A Preliminary Report on Analyses of Classroom Interaction," in *Teaching: Vantage Points for Study*, 2nd ed., ed. Ronald T. Hyman (Philadelphia: J. B. Lippincott Co., 1974), p. 186.

c. Support your statement that chemical warfare is O.K. if we are bombed by an enemy.

These questions are all categorized as evaluative in that to verify the value judgments made we need to know the criteria upon which they are based. You may be able to describe the acts performed by President Lyndon Johnson, and another person may acknowledge your description as accurate. In order for people to agree with your claim, however, that Johnson was an excellent president, they need to know your criteria for what constitutes an excellent president. Without knowing the criteria, we cannot verify the evaluation of Johnson as excellent.

The question concerning your action if you were President Kennedy is also evaluative. This question essentially seeks your opinion but sets limitations. The conditions are, of course, impossible ones because they set contrary-to-fact possibilities. You simply aren't, nor could you ever be, President Kennedy. Nevertheless, the question asks you to suppose that you are and then to give your *personal belief* on a policy matter. It is not asking you to *describe* possible consequences. That is the fundamental difference between this *opinion question* framed with hypothetical, impossible conditions, and the empirical, *contrary-to-fact* question about Watergate and McGovern asked earlier.

Note that it is possible to give a value judgment without reasons to support it. Thus, it is possible and appropriate for you to answer the question "Who is your favorite twentieth century American novelist?" with one word—"Faulkner." The question does not ask for criteria or reasons. You state your personal opinion about American novelists without giving any reasons to support it. In your answer to the previously asked question concerning the legalization of pot, however, you must give reasons since the question specifically calls for them. In your response you must give your opinion *and* your justifications.

Metaphysical.

Questions in this category ask you to give responses that state your metaphysical or theological beliefs. Such questions deal in some way or other with God or the after-life. For example,

a. Is God dead or alive?
b. Where do wicked people go after their death?
c. Does God reward the righteous person who gives to charity?

These questions are all categorized as metaphysical because they all involve faith. There is as yet no mutually agreeable way to verify the answers. Some people claim that it is impossible or unnecessary to verify them. In either case, the element of faith exists. Either you accept the statement on faith or you do not. Metaphysical questions are rare in the public schools because of the separation of church and state in our country. Such questions are more common in schools supported by religious groups. But even in parochial schools metaphysical questions may be rare. We shall therefore eliminate them from discussion from this point forward.

Let us now review the types of questions used in the formation of our categories. We can use these tentative categories to form a short or expanded set of categories. Depending on the situation for which we are categorizing, we will use whichever set suits our purposes better.

Short Set of three Categories

1.   Definitional
2.   Empirical
3.   Evaluative

Expanded Set of five Categories

A. Definitional   **1.** Definitions

B. Empirical   **2.** Facts—Specific or General

3. Relations between Facts (comparisons, purposes, and explanations giving causes, consequences, predictions, or sequences)

C. Evaluative   **4.** Opinions

5. Justifications of Opinions

It is important to keep in mind that we categorize a question according to the response it seeks to elicit and not according to its form. We know what type of response to expect by understanding the question. Obviously, we need to know the context of the question in order to understand it. The question "Who else?" is meaningless by itself. It has meaning only when we know what preceded it in the teaching situation. For example,

Question:	Name the Presidents since World War II.
Response:	Eisenhower and Kennedy.
Question:	Who else?
Response:	Um, Johnson, Truman, and Nixon.

From this short section of dialogue we understand that "Who else?" means "Name some other Presidents since World War II." Therefore, we categorize it as an empirical question asking for a specific fact. Similarly, if the next utterance is "And?" then we categorize that too as an empirical question expecting a specific fact even though the question is asked in a highly shortened form. The context signifies to us that the speaker is cutting the question short and relying on the respondent to fill in the omitted part. The full question would be "And name another President since World War II." In short, we must understand the question and then determine what cognitive process it expects in order to categorize it properly.

The importance of this approach to categorizing questions lies in the fact that it allows us to view the thinking process in a variety of ways. Once we realize that it is possible to make distinctions among questions based on a solid conceptual base, we no longer assume that all questions are alike. Different types of questions—definitional, empirical, evaluative—take us into different realms of meaning. By asking a variety of questions and considering the responses in terms of the verification needed for them we introduce the respondents to a fuller view of the world in general. In this way we become aware of the different types of questions, and we become adept at responding in the appropriate manner.

According to research which used categories based on the concept of verification, the empirical mode of thought predominates in classrooms.[6] Smith and Meux report the predominance of the empirical mode in the secondary level mathematics, science, social studies, and English classrooms that they observed. In research dealing with the topic of world trade, Bellack and his associates report that over eighty percent of the questions were empirical.[7]

Just why this emphasis on the empirical mode occurs is not apparent from the data collected by the researchers. Nevertheless, it is clear that a balance of opportunities for students to practice different modes of thinking is not available. Students respond to the questions asked and thus perform the thinking processes required of them by their teachers. Students probably do not ask for a variety of thinking processes because the model presented to them by their teachers does not suggest the possibility.

Use the categories, their definitions, and their examples to classify the questions which follow in Practice Exercise 1. The practice exercise will serve as a review/feedback device which should be helpful to you.

---

[6]B. Othanel Smith and Milton Meux, "A Study of the Logic of Teaching," in *Teaching: Vantage Points for Study*, ed. Ronald T. Hyman (Philadelphia: J. B. Lippincott Co., 1968), pp. 116-17.
[7]Bellack and others, *The Language of the Classroom*, p. 112.

Practice Exercise 1
Question Types: Cognitive Processes

Use The Expanded Set of 5 Categories to classify these questions. Write your decision to the left of each question.

_____ 1. Q: Why does Hamlet stage a play within a play?
            Res: To see the queen's reaction.
_____ 2. Q: Another reason?
            Res: To see the king's reaction.
_____ 3. Q: What's the difference between our Congress and the British Parliament?
            Res: I don't know.
            Res: The House of Lords is very weak.
_____ 4. Q : What else?
            Res: The Prime Minister is a member of the House of Commons and our President is not a member of Congress.
_____ 5. Q: What do you mean by "Prime Minister"?
            Res: The Prime Minister is the head of their government.
_____ 6. Q: Who is the current Prime Minister of Britain— Wilson or Callaghan?
_____ 7. Q: If we had lost the last world war to the Nazis, what would our country be like today?
            Res: Rotten.
            Res: We'd all be speaking German.
            Res: We'd all be studying about the great leader Adolf Hitler.
_____ 8. Q: Accepting this and what you know from other wars, what conclusion can you draw about the victors and the losers in a war?
_____ 9. Q: Why were the Beatles so popular in the 1960s?
            Res: They brought in a new style of music.
_____10. Q: If the Beatles come back, will they be a success again?
            Res: If the Beatles come back, they'll be a flop 'cause they're out of date now.

——11. Q: Why are the Beatles still your favorite rock group?

——12. Q: What do the birds that stay in the North eat during the winter?

Res: Seeds left on the trees.

Res: Lots of people feed them.

——13. Q: Do cardinals fly South?

Res: No.

——14. Q: Don't robins fly South?

——15. Q: If you mix a jar of blue paint and a jar of yellow paint, what will happen—besides you getting all messed up with paint?

Res: You'll get two jars of green paint.

——16. Q: How do you divide 6732 by 84?

Res: Put 6732 in the inside and 84 on the outside. Then you put 84 into 673 and it goes 8 times . . .

——17. Q: If it doesn't divide evenly, do you carry it to two decimal places?

Res: Carry it to two decimal places.

——18. Q: If you were Shakespeare, would you want to write for our contemporary theater?

——19. Q: If Shakespeare were alive today, would he write comedies or tragedies?

Res: Both.

——20. Q: What medium do you think Shakespeare would write for?

Res: Television, because he always tried to appeal to the mass public.

Author's Responses to Practice Exercise 1
Question Types: Cognitive Processes

1. 3, purpose or reason for staging the play.

2. 3, another purpose or reason for staging the play.

3. 3, compare and contrast the two legislatures.

4. 3, some more comparisons and contrasts.

5. 1, definition of the term Prime Minister.

6. 2, specific fact about the current situation.

7. 3, contrary-to-fact relationship.

8. 2, make a generalization on information you have.

9. 3, explain by giving causes of the popularity of the Beatles.

10. 3, what are the possible consequences of a possible future event. This is not a contrary-to-*fact* event. The possibility lies in the future; it is not factually impossible.

11. 5, give reasons for a personal preference.

12. 2, specific facts about the biology of birds.

13. 2, specific fact about cardinals.

14. 2,specific facts about robins.

15. 3, what will be the consequences of an event in the future.

16. 3, setting the sequence of procedures so as to explain the division.

17. 3, what will occur as a consequence of an event.

18. 4, personal opinion about an impossible situation; nevertheless it is a personal belief asked for.

19. 3, seeking the consequence of a contrary-to-fact event.

20. 3, seeking the consequence of a contrary-to-fact event; the question is short for, "If Shakespeare were alive today, what in terms of media and not topics would he write for?

THREE

QUESTION TYPES: OTHER CONSIDERATIONS

The previous chapter dealt with cognitive types of questions. When we consider the context of questions within teaching, it is clear that there are other factors about questions we wish to consider. This chapter will treat three main considerations—production type, information process activity, and response clue. As shown later on in Figure 3-1, these considerations cut across the cognitive categories already presented and form a grid with them.

PRODUCTION TYPE

As hinted at in an earlier chapter, we may wish to know if the respondent is recalling the answer from memory or offering a fresh response. Suppose you ask "What do you infer about the U.S. from the fact that our coins are made from copper and silver?" Only the context of the interaction will indicate whether you are asking the respondent to recall the answer from memory or you are asking the respondent to make a fresh inference. An answer that is summoned from memory is called "reproductive thinking." An answer that is created on the spot is called "productive thinking."[1]

We can apply the terms reproductive and productive thinking to each of the three main cognitive categories. It is possible for a question to elicit memory in regard to definitions, empirical statements, or evaluative matters. That is why it is not true that a student is "thinking" just because you have asked a "why" question. (The old statement "Don't ask for facts; ask them *why* if you want them to think" just doesn't hold true.) Your question "What caused the depression of the 1930s?" may indeed elicit productive thinking. But it might also elicit reproductive thinking if the student simply recalls an answer read in the text or seen in a film. In short, a question asking for reasons is no guarantee that you will elicit productive thinking and not reproductive recall.

INFORMATION-PROCESS ACTIVITY

Another consideration about a question is the information-process activity you wish the respondent to perform when responding. Every question by its nature must indicate to the respondent that a particular information-process activity is expected. As respondents to questions, we know what is expected of us because we understand how the questions are phrased. Even if the information-process activity is implicit in the structure of a question rather than explicitly stated, we readily know what process to perform.

There are three main types of information-process activity—yes/no, selection, and construction.

1. Yes/No. Questions in this category require the respondent to an-

---

[1] James J. Gallagher and Mary Jane Aschner, "A Preliminary Report on Analyses of Classroom Interaction," in *Teaching: Vantage Points for Study*, 2nd ed., ed. Ronald T. Hyman (Philadelphia: J. B. Lippincott Co., 1974), pp. 183-87.

swer yes, no, or one of the verbal equivalents such as sure, certainly not, uh-uh, or hm-hm.

  a. Is it presently legal to execute a convicted murderer?
  b. Did you vote for Carter in 1976?
  c. Is 16 the square root of 225?

2. Selection. Questions in this category require the respondent to select from the alternatives given. There may be two, three, or more items to select from.

  a. Did you vote for Carter or Ford in 1976?
  b. Is 16 the square root of 225, 256, 266, or 276?
  c. Is sulphuric acid H_2SO_4, H_2S, or H_2SO?

3. Construction. Questions in this category require the respondent to construct the response based on the meaning of the questions. The respondent cannot answer yes/no or select from the alternatives offered.

  a. Who was the President after Eisenhower?
  b. What game do you want to play after your snack?
  c. Give your opinion about rationing home heating oil.

There are some variations in these three types of information-process activity which involve combining the basic types. For example, "Can you tell me what time it is?" is structurally a yes/no question. When most people ask a question like this, however, they do not expect a yes/no response. What they expect is a construction response that tells them the time. For this reason the question is not precise and is somewhat misleading. For our purposes we shall stick with the three main information-process activities.

The importance of considering what the information-process activity is lies in the fact that, according to our research, teachers and students ask different types of questions. In a study of teacher-student interaction in fifteen high school economics classes, the following distribution of question types was found.[2]

[2]Arno A. Bellack, Herbert M. Kliebard, Ronald T. Hyman, and Frank L. Smith, Jr., *The Language of the Classroom* (New York: Teachers College Press, 1966), p. 114.

	Percent of Teachers' Questions	Percent of Students' Questions
Yes/No	12.5	60.5
Selection	2.0	4.3
Construction	79.2	33.9
Construction-Yes/No	6.3	1.3
Total	100.0	100.0

These data show that in the observed classes the students most often asked yes/no questions. About four out of five of the teachers' questions required the students to construct their own responses, whereas only one-eighth of the questions required students to respond yes or no. The different percentages of teacher questions and student questions may be a reflection of role, age, or both.

Although it is not apparent from the data why the students preferred yes/no questions, it is possible to suggest an explanation. According to O'Connor, yes/no questions and selection questions with two stated alternatives are the most precise types of questions.[3] These types of questions offer the respondent a choice between two possibilities, although "I don't know," "neither," and "both" are always acceptable alternative answers. There cannot be less than two alternatives because with only one possible choice there is no decision for the respondent to make and hence there is no question to ask. As the number of alternatives increases from two to three or more, the question becomes less precise. The larger the number of alternatives, the more general the question and less comfortable the students feel about the expected response.

In addition, children tend to look at people and events in terms of black and white. Young people simply are not mature enough to cope with the gray area between the two extremes

---

[3]D. J. O'Connor, *An Introduction to the Philosophy of Education* (London: Routledge and Kegan Paul, 1957), p. 32.

of a dichotomy.[4] It may be that they ask yes/no questions which provide resonses they can handle in terms of precision.

RESPONSE CLUE

A third major consideration of questions involves the response clue or clues offered to the respondent within the question itself. There are five types of response clues which aid the respondent, and more than one may be in a given question.

Wh-Words.

Questions often give clues to aid the respondent. Clues offered by such interrogative words as when, why, what, who, and how many tell the respondent to answer in terms of time, reasons, people, and number. These wh- words often form the essence of the question.

Parallel Terms.

Questions with this type of response clue indicate to the respondent that the expected response is similar to some previous response. The questioner expects more of what is already available and clues the respondent to that expectation with such words as "another," "and," "else," and "something else." These vague words, as mentioned earlier, take on meaning only within the context of the interaction.

Teacher:	Name a President since World War II.
Student:	Eisenhower.
Teacher:	Who else?
Student:	Johnson.
Teacher:	And?
Student:	Nixon.

[4]Bruno Bettelheim, "Their Country, Right or Wrong," *Ladies' Home Journal*, 85 (June 1968), pp. 35-38.

Note the contextual meaning of the parallel term in the brief dialogue above.

Cited Terms.

Questions with this type of response clue indicate to the respondent the framework within which to respond. The clues may indicate a general category to be specified further or may specify the correct terms to use.

a. Who are the best authors of mysteries, in terms of nationality?
b. State your reasons for supporting the legalization of pot—give legal reasons, please.

Excluded Terms.

Questions with this type of response clue indicate to the respondent what is *not* to be used in responding. The terms indicating what is to be excluded may offer help as to the level of the expected response. Such excluding terms include besides, other than, and excluding.

a. What are some good woods, besides cherry, to use in building your furniture?
b. Excluding NaCl, which is common table salt, name three salts we have worked with in this unit.

Leading the Respondent.

Questions with this type of response clue give a strong implied clue to the respondent about the correct expected response. Leading questions call for the yes/no information-process activity. The leading clue involves "it is, isn't it?" or some variation of this phrase, either in the positive or negative form. In effect, the question makes a statement and *leads* the respondent to agree with it. Of course the respondent may disagree, but the implication favors agreement.

a. Isn't "mi" the third note of the scale?

b. The formula for the area of a rectangle is length times width, isn't it?

c. Apes aren't considered part of Homo sapiens, are they?

The importance of response clues stems from the fundamental idea that the questioner is asking the question to get an answer. Since the point of the question is to get a response, it is sensible for the questioner to aid the respondent with clues so as to facilitate appropriate responses. For example, if you wish to know who are the best basketball players in the world, then it is certainly sensible and legitimate for you to offer a clue about type of response desired rather than play the game of "you read my mind and figure out what I mean by my question." For example, you may ask "Who, in terms of nationality, are the best basketball players in the world?" If you don't include the phrase "in terms of nationality" as a response leader, you will probably get the names of specific players rather than the name of the country from which they come.

Obviously, and especially in an oral-test situation, there may be times when you wish to avoid giving clues. There may even be times when you wish to find out how the respondent interprets the question within the context of the teaching situation. This is not, however, a common practice. Most of the time the questioner knows what type of response is desired, but this does not necessarily mean that the questioner knows the answer. There is, therefore, no sense in playing cat and mouse with the respondent.

Furthermore, as a teacher you know the strengths and weaknesses of your students. The addition of response clues to your questions offers you an excellent way of personalizing your questions. With this subtle and sophisticated method you can facilitate a student's participation in the interaction of teaching. The deliberate use of response clues is the sign of a knowledgeable questioner.

Let us review the three main considerations and their ten subpoints which we can apply to questions regardless of the cognitive process required to respond:

1. Production Type
   a. Reproductive
   b. Productive
2. Information-Process Activity
   a. Yes/No
   b. Selection
   c. Construction
3. Response Clues
   a. Wh- Words
   b. Parallel Terms
   c. Cited Terms
   d. Excluded Terms
   e. Leading the Respondent

With these considerations in mind, we may form a grid (as in Figure 3-1) of question types.

Try classifying the questions used earlier according to the considerations of production type, information-process activity, and response clue. The questions and instructions appear in Practice Exercise 2.

Practice Exercise 2
Question Types: Other Considerations

Classify each question below according to Production Type, Information-Process Activity, and Response Clue. For Response Clue you may have more than one clue used in a given question. Also, it will be difficult if not impossible at times to classify these questions according to Production Type since the overall context for these questions is not known to you. Therefore, classify carefully and know ahead of time that there is leeway due to the uncertainty of the context. Write your responses to the left of each question.

COGNITIVE PROCESS		PRODUCTION TYPE		INFORMATION-PROCESS ACTIVITY				RESPONSE CLUE				
		Productive	Repro- ductive	Yes/No	Selection	Construc- tion	Wh– Inter- rogative Words	Parallel Words	Cited Terms	Excluded Terms	Leading the Respondent
Short Set	Expanded Set										
Definitional	Definitions										
Empirical	Facts										
	Relations between facts										
Evaluative	Opinions										
	Justifica- tions										

Figure 3-1   Question Grid

_____ **1.** Q: Why does Hamlet stage a play within a play?

Res: To see the queen's reaction.

_____ **2.** Q: Another reason?

Res: To see the king's reaction.

_____ **3.** Q: What's the difference between our Congress and the British Parliament?

Res: I don't know.

Res: The House of Lords is very weak.

_____ **4.** Q: What else?

Res: The Prime Minister is a member of the House of Commons and our President is not a member of Congress.

_____ **5.** Q: What do you mean by "Prime Minister"?

Res: The Prime Minister is the head of their government.

_____ **6.** Q: Who is the current Prime Minister of Britain—Wilson or Callaghan?

_____ **7.** Q: If we had lost the last world war to the Nazis, what would our country be like today?

Res: Rotten.

Res: We'd all be speaking German.

Res: We'd all be studying about the great leader Adolf Hitler.

_____ **8.** Q: Accepting this and what you know from other wars, what conclusion can you draw about the victors and the losers in a war?

_____ **9.** Q: Why were the Beatles so popular in the 1960s?

Res: They brought in a new style of music.

_____**10.** Q: If the Beatles come back, will they be a success again?

Res: If the Beatles come back, they'll be a flop 'cause they're out of date now.

_____**11.** Q: Why are the Beatles still your favorite rock group?

_____**12.** Q: What do the birds that stay in the North eat during the winter?

Res: Seeds left on the trees.

Res: Lots of people feed them.

_____**13.** Q: Do cardinals fly South?

Res: No.

_____ **14.** Q: Don't robins fly South?

_____ **15.** Q: If you mix a jar of blue paint and a jar of yellow paint, what will happen—besides you getting all messed up with paint?

Res: You'll get two jars of green paint.

_____ **16.** Q: How do you divide 6732 by 84?

Res: Put 6732 in the inside and 84 on the outside. Then you put 84 into 673 and it goes 8 times...

_____ **17.** Q: If it doesn't divide evenly, do you carry it to two decimal places?

Res: Carry it to two decimal places.

_____ **18.** Q: If you were Shakespeare, would you want to write for our contemporary theater?

_____ **19.** Q: If Shakespeare were alive today, would he write comedies or tragedies?

Res: Both.

_____ **20.** Q: What medium do you think Shakespeare would write for?

Res: Television, because he always tried to appeal to the mass public.

Author's Responses to Practice Exercise
Question Types: Other Considerations

1. Construction; Wh-; productive.
2. Construction; parallel terms; productive.
3. Construction; Wh-; productive.
4. Construction; parallel terms; productive.
5. Construction; Wh-; reproductive.
6. Selection; Wh-; reproductive.
7. Construction; Wh-; productive.
8. Construction; Wh-; productive.
9. Construction; Wh-; productive.
10. Yes/No; productive.
11. Construction; Wh-; productive.

12. Construction; Wh-; productive.
13. Yes/No; reproductive.
14. Yes/No; Leading the Respondent; reproductive.
15. Construction; Excluded terms.
16. Construction; reproductive.
17. Yes/No; reproductive.
18. Yes/No; productive.
19. Selection; productive.
20. Construction; Cited terms, Excluded terms; productive.

FOUR

FIVE GENERAL STRATEGIES FOR ASKING QUESTIONS

This chapter offers five overall strategies for asking questions. Obviously, no single strategy could or should apply to all teaching situations. The context of time, space, and the development of the students is always changing. What worked yesterday with one class may not work next week with another group of students studying the same topic. Nevertheless, once you have a knowledge of alternative strategies, it is easier to modify previous approaches to fit a current situation.

THE MIXED STRATEGY

The simplest questioning strategy, the mixed strategy, suggests that you mix the types of questions you ask. This sounds simple, yet many teachers do not mix their questions well. Teachers generally ask the same type of question without achieving a recognizable mixture. Thus, one type of question predominates.

In a study conducted with student teachers, Davis and Tinsley classified questions into the nine categories of their

Teacher-Pupil Question Inventory. The forty-four student teachers and their students asked more "memory" questions (1313) than all other questions (2520) combined.[1] Gall reviewed a half-century of reserach on teacher questioning and drew the similar conclusion that "about 60% of teachers' questions require students to recall facts. . . ."[2] In a study conducted at Columbia University we found that 79.5% of the teachers' (and 84.3% of the students') questions were in the empirical mode of thought. Of the remaining teacher questions, 15.7% were in the definitional mode and only 4.7% were in the evaluative mode. Furthermore, 79.2% of the teachers' questions in that study were of the construction type in regard to information-process activity.[3]

What the reserach on questioning shows is that teachers ask a limited variety of questions. Whatever the cause, it is sufficient to say that if students are to achieve the general social and individual goals commonly advocated by educators and parents alike it is necessary to vary the types of questions asked. If the goals are varied, then the type of questions asked must also be varied. This will ensure that the students can perform the cognitive tasks necessary to achieve the goals.

The mixed strategy guides you toward the goal of pluralism. The first step is to realize that there are five different cognitive processes within the three modes of thought, each with three other main considerations. Thus the possibilities for variety are significant. See the question grid in Figure 3-1.

The second step is to recognize that in teaching there is a need for all types of questions. For example, the oft-maligned factual memory question is not *ipso facto* a bad question. Stu-

[1]O.L. Davis, Jr., and Drew C. Tinsley, "Cognitive Objectives Revealed by Classroom Questions Asked by Social Studies Student Teachers," in *Teaching: Vantage Points for Study*, ed. Ronald T. Hyman (Philadelphia: J.B. Lippincott Co., 1968), p. 142.

[2]Meredith D. Gall, "The Use of Questions in Teaching," *Review of Educational Research*, 40, no. 5 (December, 1970), p. 713.

[3]Arno A. Bellack and others, *The Language of the Classroom* (New York: Teachers College Press, 1966), pp. 112-14.

dents must build on what they recall in order to respond to and ask other types of questions. Thus, it is not a matter of "good and bad" in regard to questions, but rather a matter of "appropriate and inappropriate."

The third step is to recognize that there is no absolute in regard to the appropriateness of a question. Appropriateness is relative to time and student. For example, a question requesting an explanation of a person's action ("Why did you heat the test tube over the Bunsen burner?") may be inappropriate at the beginning of a lesson but not halfway through it. Such a question may simply be too early in the sequence when asked at the start of the lesson. Moreover, what is appropriate to ask one student may be inappropriate with another. To a student who has been absent for several days or to one who has been struggling to keep up with the class, it is inappropriate to ask a question eliciting a conclusion based on a wealth of available data. ("From our discussions and the graphs showing precinct voting statistics, what do you conclude about the city voters in the 1976 elections?") Such students are probably not prepared at that moment for such a powerful question. The threat caused by the cognitive demands of that question may be too much for those students.

For students who enjoy participating but who need to be made to feel secure enough to venture a response that they feel will not be embarrassing, a nonthreatening question is appropriate. A question that has a response clue such as a parallel or cited term or a question that calls for the presentation of material to add to the available data is less threatening. ("In regard to the President, what else do our charts tell us about how the blacks in New York City voted during the 1976 election?")

Note that this question is not a recall question. In such a situation, a recall question may be a subtle negative reinforcement of the student's nonparticipation in the ongoing topic. The teacher does not wish to convey the negative message "You can't do it; you can't participate meaningfully; therefore, you get the 'baby' question." The question should offer the student an opportunity to participate meaningfully but within a nonthreatening context. In our example there are response clues (cited and parallel terms). The question calls for reading specific data from a chart so as to keep the cognitive demand light. The cognitive demand of reading data from a chart is less than that required to draw a conclusion based on an analysis of the available data.

The key to the mixed strategy is variety. It may well be that some questions appear to be out of logical sequence according to some other strategy. (Several other strategies shall be offered in the pages that follow.) Some questions may be inappropriate to a given student at a given time. It is impossible to be on target at all times. Nevertheless, variety of questions offers the students an opportunity to expand the range of their thinking with you as teacher. Students need to respond to a variety of questions to develop cognitively and to enhance their own questioning ability.

Even within each of the five cognitive processes, further variety is possible and desirable. For example, category 3 in the expanded set of 5 categories (see Chapter 2) calls for explanations. In this category we place questions that attempt to find out *why* events happened. But *why* questions do not exhaust the possibilities for explanation. It is also possible, desirable, and often preferable to explain events in terms of *how*. You can ask "How did this event come to pass?" and "How does a heart function?" to vary the types of explaining students perform. A *how* question is quite different from a *why* question, which is a frequent teacher question. A similar case can be made for defining. I shall develop this point further (see Chapter 6) when I offer exercises in seeking a variety of cognitive processes.

Note the variety of questions in the following short extract. As a careful reader you will be able to infer something about the particular students involved. The entries are numbered for easy referral.

1.	**Teacher:**	I took a look at your "garden" when I walked by it before. What did you plant in it?
2.	**John:**	Vegetables.
3.	**Teacher:**	Did *you* plant the lettuce or the carrots, Sam?
4.	**Sam:**	I planted the lettuce and the carrots.
5.	**Pat:**	I planted the radishes.
6.	**Teacher:**	When the first green parts start showing how will you tell one plant from the other?
7.	**Pat:**	By where we planted them—front and back.
8.	**Teacher:**	True enough. Besides position, how will you tell them apart as they *grow*?
9.	**Sam:**	Well, their leaves are different, I guess. We'll look it up on the packages of seeds where there are pictures. How else?
10.	**John:**	There ought to be a different germinating and developing time, too. By checking our time log we can count days and see which grew first and fastest.
11.	**Teacher:**	If only one vegetable grows, which one would you prefer it to be?
12.	**Pat:**	The carrots.
13.	**Sam:**	Carrots.
14.	**John:**	Corn.
15.	**Teacher:**	Thanks—if it turns out to be radishes, let me know and I'll help eat them. In the meantime, let me know what's going on as the plants develop.

Practice Exercise 3
Mixed Strategy

Refer to the short "garden" extract which precedes this practice exercise. Each of the utterances is numbered for convenience in refering to them. Write your responses to each of the nine items below.

1. At point 3, suggest an opinion question that the teacher could have asked.
2. At point 3, suggest another question different from the specific fact question that is there and the opinion question you formulated above.
3. At point 6, suggest a causal question (category 3) with selection as the information-process activity.
4. At point 6, suggest another specific fact question with parallel terms as a response clue.
5. At point 6, suggest a generalization or conclusion question with yes/no as the information process activity.
6. At point 6, suggest a compare/contrast question.
7. At point 11, suggest a contrary-to-fact consequence question.
8. Make up as many other questions as you can so as to demonstrate the possibility for variety.
9. Assume that you are Sam at point 9. Ask one question of the teacher and one of John or Pat.

Author's Responses to Practice Exercise 3
Mixed Strategy

For this practice exercise there are no right or wrong answers. Below are some possibilities. Compare your answers to those listed below.

1. a. Do you like to eat vegetables?
   b. Which is your favorite vegetable?
2. a. If they grow, will you eat them or give them away?
   b. Why did you plant vegetables?
   c. What's the difference between the vegetables you planted and the ones you eat at home?
3. a. Does the light or the water cause the plants to bloom early?
   b. What was the main cause of your success last year with your garden—warm weather or good fertilizer?

4. a.   What else did you plant?

  b.   Any others?

5. a.   Is it true that all the vegetables you planted are standard ones?

  b.   Can we say that there are no exotic plants or herbs in your garden?

6. a.   In what ways are radishes and carrots similar?

  b.   Besides the obvious color difference, what's the difference between carrots and lettuce?

7. a.   If carrots demanded a dry and sandy soil, what would you have done?

  b.   If radishes were sweet, would you have planted more of them?

8. a.   What do you mean by vegetable?

  b.   If you plant vegetables indoors during the winter, do they grow as fast as vegetables outside in the summer?

9. a.   Can you tell them apart just from the leaves?

  b.   Did you save the package envelopes, Pat?

PEAKS STRATEGY AND PLATEAUS STRATEGY

The second and third strategies derive their names from the visual effect of charting questions according to two different progressions. In the *peaks strategy* you ask a student a question and then continue asking that student a series of related questions before going to another student. For example, you may ask a student named Pat, "When was Watergate?" (Simple Fact.) You follow with "Compare Watergate with another government scandal." (Comparison of Facts.) You may then ask "What caused the Watergate scandal?" (Causes.) Your final question may be "What conclusions about American society do you reach from your examination of the Watergate affair?" (Conclusion, generalization, or inference from the Facts.) Now you begin to question Chris, another student, in a similar manner, moving from fact to comparison to causes to conclusions. You might then move on to Sandy and Lenny, two other students.

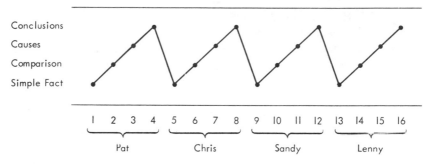

Figure 4-1.   Peaks Strategy of Questioning

When we plot this progression of questions for our four hypothetical students, Pat, Chris, Sandy, and Lenny, the figure resembles a picture of peaks. (See Figure 4–1) The vertical lines represent the four types of questions. The horizontal line represents the sixteen questions that you asked in groups of four questions per student.

Below is a short extract from a three-step peaks strategy used by a teacher on the topic of "bicycles as machines." Try to identify the progression of questions asked by the teacher as you consider the development of the interaction.

Teacher:	Now that it's spring again and our minds turn to the outdoors, let's tie in our study of machines with a popular vehicle—the bike. Name a part of a bike.
Mel:	The chain.
Teacher:	What's its purpose?
Mel:	It gets the wheel to move. It connects the pedal to the wheel.
Teacher:	Do you conclude that the chain is necessary for the bike? That is, do you really need it?
Mel:	Yeah, you need it. You can't go without it unless you're coasting downhill or someone's pushing you. But then you die out and stop.
Teacher:	Let's discuss another part, Andrea.
Andrea:	The brakes.
Teacher:	What's the purpose of the brakes?
Andrea:	To slow down or to stop you.

Teacher: Is the conclusion that you need the brakes?
Andrea: Well, I think you do. I wouldn't ride a bike without brakes. But Yael's older brother showed her this article about racing bikes and they don't have any brakes at all.

(The teacher and students proceed similarly through nine other parts of the bicycle.)

Teacher: Well, now that we've talked about many parts of the bike, would someone please offer a generalization about the parts of your bikes?
Mel: Simple. You need some parts, but you don't need others.
Yael: I want to add that it depends on whose bike it is.

In the example, the teacher carefully asks each student a series of three different questions:

1. Name a part of your bike (specific fact).
2. What is the purpose or function of that part of the bike (explain purpose)?
3. Do you conclude that the part is necessary to the bike (draw conclusion?

After discussing many parts in this way, one student per bike part, the teacher asks for a general, overall conclusion based on all of the comments made.

In the *plateaus strategy* you ask a series of questions of the same type to the four students before moving on to the next type of question. For example, you ask for some facts about Watergate from each of the students. You then request comparisons with another government scandal. Then you seek the causes of Watergate. Finally you ask the students to draw some conclusions based on the available Watergate data. The plateaus questions may be the same questions as the peaks questions.

When we plot this progression of questions with our four

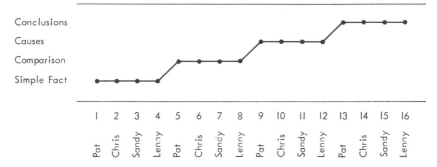

Figure 4-2   Plateaus Strategy of Questioning

hypothetical students, Pat, Chris, Sandy, and Lenny, the figure resembles a picture of plateaus (See Figure 4–2.) On the vertical line are the four types of questions. On the horizontal line are the sixteen questions asked in groups of four each.

The following is a short extract from a plateaus strategy with the same topic of "bicycles as machines." Note the progression of questions and the nature of the interaction.

Teacher:	Now that it's spring again and our minds turn to the outdoors, let's tie in our study of machines with a popular vehicle—the bike. Name some parts of a bicycle.
Mel:	The wheel and chain.
Andrea:	Brake, seat, handlebars, fenders.
Teacher:	We've got six so far. What else?
Yael:	Spokes, tire, inner tube, bell . . .
Mel:	Pedal.
Teacher:	That gives us eleven which I've listed on the board. In order now, what's the purpose of the wheel?
Mel:	To go 'round and make you go forward.
Teacher:	The chain?
Yael:	To get the wheel to move. It connects the pedal to the wheel.
Teacher:	The brake?
Sandy:	Obvious, to stop the bike so you don't kill yourself.

(The teacher and students proceed similarly through the remaining 8 parts.)

Teacher:	You've done a super job of giving the purpose of each of these parts. Keep those purposes in mind and tell me what you think about the necessity of each part for your bike. That is, which parts do you really need?
Yael:	Well, I think you really need the wheel, the chain, the handlbars, and the pedal. That's all.
Andrea:	You need the brakes, too.
Yael:	No you don't. My older brother showed me this article about racing bikes and they don't have any brakes at all.
Mel:	Yeah but we need brakes on *our* bikes. We're not racing.
Yael:	O.K.
Teacher:	What do you conclude about the seat?
Andrea:	I think we need it. You can't stand up and pedal all day; it's impossible. You might be able to do it for a short while, but you really need a seat.
Teacher:	What about the fenders, the spokes, tires, inner tubes, and bell?
Sandy:	The spokes, tires, and inner tubes are all parts of the wheel. They make up the wheel so we need them. But the fenders and bell are not really needed. You can get along without them. Mel doesn't have any fenders at all on his beat-up "tank."
Teacher:	We've talked about each of the eleven—
Andrea:	Wait—if you claim that you need the brakes, then I think you need the bell, too. My father won't let me ride without one. He's a bug on safety.
Sandy:	But you don't *really* need it. You can whistle or shout. It's not like the brakes, it's different. I say no.
Teacher:	We've talked about all eleven. Now, is there one big generalization you can make about the parts of your bikes?
Mel:	Simple. You need some parts, you don't need others.
Yael:	I want to add that it depends on whose bike it is.

In the example strategy the teacher carefully stays with the same type of question before moving to another type in the progression. The teacher stays with one level of questioning until enough discussion has been generated at that level. At one point the teacher repeats the first type of question by asking a question containing parallel terms as a response clue. The question succeeds in eliciting five more bicycle parts. Only after conclusions are offered for each of the listed parts does the teacher ask for the general conclusion.

Note that from one peaks or plateaus strategy to another the number, type, and order of questions may vary. In the two examples used the questions were simple fact, comparison, cause, and conclusion. In the two extracts used as illustrations the questions were simple fact, explain purpose, and conclusion. In another strategy you may ask a cluster of simple facts, consequence of event, consequence of nonevent, opinion, and justify opinion. The number, type, and order of the questions asked depends on your understanding of the students and the topic at hand.

In a pilot study reporting on the classroom frequency of these two strategies we found that teachers used the peaks strategy much more than the plateaus strategy. We observed six volunteer teachers who were not aware of the focus of observation. The six teachers were in the areas of Social Studies, English, and Science in a new suburban New York City high school, grades seven through eleven. There was no attempt (or possibility) to achieve a controlled sampling of teachers in that school. The results show that about ninety percent of the questioning patterns were strictly within the empirical mode of thought and were of the peaks strategy type.[4]

Each of these strategies has its advantages and its place in teaching. When you are concerned with group participation and attention, the plateaus strategy is the one to use.[5] Stu-

---

[4]Ronald T. Hyman, "Questioning in the Classroom," *Resources in Education*, September, 1977. ERIC #ED138551.

[5]Jack R. Fraenkel, *How To Teach about Values* (Englewood Cliffs, N.J.: Prentice-Hall, Inc., 1977), p. 93.

dents who are developing a wealth of facts to explain and/or generalize from develop a group attitude and interdependency. Students are more willing to offer explanations and generalizations because they have a stake in what has been offered up to that point. Because of this, there is more participation on each subsequent plateau.

You should also use the plateaus strategy when you wish to emphasize that generalizations and conclusions need to be based on a cluster of facts, comparisons, or causes. This is why you try to elicit a group of facts, a group of comparisons based on the available group of facts, a group of opinions, and so forth before beginning to elicit conclusions or generalizations. The exact number of facts, causes, opinions, or conclusions depends on your understanding of the teaching situation. The number of simple facts needed in a class's fact group may range from three to fifty or more.

When you are concerned mainly with the thinking process of a given student, the peaks strategy is the one to use.[6] You may wish to probe with a particular student once you have that student involved and participating. You go from facts to comparisons, causes, and conclusions with one student because you wish to see that student develop the topic individually. Given that you are not threatening the student with an interrogating tone, the student should be willing to move to different types of questions. This is because the student will have everybody's attention as well as having a personal stake in the discussion.

The peaks strategy has a small variation which you can use if you wish to emphasize the topic under study rather than an individual student's thinking processes. Instead of pursuing the series of questions with one student at a time, you can switch students as you switch question type. You can either select the student for whom the question is most appropriate or allow volunteers to respond. In this way the question itself becomes important as the means for dealing with the topic.

[6]Ibid., p. 94.

This will permit more students to participate and reduce any threat which a student might feel from having to answer an entire series of questions.

The plateaus strategy also has a small variation which you can use if you wish to emphasize the strengths of a particular student. Instead of allowing many students to respond to a question of a particular cognitive-process type, you ask one student to concentrate on the process. For example, one student may provide all the specific parts of bicycles, one student may give all the purposes of these parts, and one may give all the conclusions about the necessity of each part. Here too you can either select the student for whom the question is most appropriate or allow volunteers to respond. This variation allows the students to perform the cognitive process with which they are most comfortable.

In some teaching situations a three- or four-question peaks or plateaus strategy may take an entire lesson. In other situations, such a sequence of questions may last a few minutes and become a portion of an entire lesson or a still larger strategy. The length depends upon the preparation of the students, the willingness of the teacher to encourage student expansion, and the topic.

A peaks strategy and a plateaus strategy may become elements of a larger inductive or deductive strategy of questioning. I shall turn to inductive and deductive strategies after you complete Practice Exercise 4 on peaks and plateaus.

Practice Exercise 4
Peaks Strategy and Plateaus Strategy

For this exercise refer to the two previous extracts which dealt with bicycles by using the peaks strategy and the plateaus strategy. See pages 40–42.

Recall that in each of these two extracts:

a. Question 1 asks the respondent to state a specific fact.
b. Question 2 asks the respondent to explain something by giving its purpose or function.
c. Question 3 asks the respondent to draw a conclusion.
d. Question 4 asks the respondent to draw an overall conclusion (make a generalization).

Write your responses to each of the four items below.

1. Suggest a substitute for question 3 which will still provide a progression of questions from question 1 to question 4.
2. Suggest a substitute for question 2 which will still provide you with a strategic link between question 1 and question 3.
3. Suggest a three to five question progression for a peaks or plateaus strategy on the topic "The Bicycle Redesigned."
4. Suggest three to seven question progression for a peaks or plateaus strategy on the topic "The Bike as the Ideal Vehicle in a World Short of Gasoline Energy."

Author's Responses to Practice Exercise 4
Peaks Strategy and Plateaus Strategy

For this practice exercise there are no right and wrong answers. Below are some possibilities. Compare your answers to those listed below.

1. a. If you were to be changed into a bike by the Fairy of the Highway, what bike part would you choose to become? (Consequence of nonevent.)
   b. Rate each bike part on a scale of one to ten regarding its necessity to the bike. A rating of one means it's not necessary. A rating of ten means it is absolutely necessary. (Opinion.)
2. a. How does this part contribute to your safety when you ride your bike? (Explain procedure.)
   b. Rank order each part of the bike, in terms of importance, from one to eleven. If parts are tied for a particular rank, average them for that rank. For example, if three parts are tied for rank two, your first five ranks will read 1-3-3-3-5. (Opinion.)

3. a. List four important parts of a bike which have similar parts in a car. (Specific fact.)
    b. Compare these bike parts with the car parts in any way you wish. (Compare.)
    c. If you were hired as a bike designer, what changes would you make in these bike parts? (Consequence of event.)
4. a. List three or more possible new uses for bikes in industry and transportation. (Specific fact.)
    b. Propose a new policy or law that will encourage the use of bikes by businesses and private citizens. (Opinion.)
    c. Give reasons to support this new policy or law. (Justify opinion.)
    d. Explain how you would go about gaining support for this policy or law to get it adopted. (Explain procedure.)

INDUCTIVE STRATEGY AND DEDUCTIVE STRATEGY

Many people seem to have trouble distinguishing between the processes of induction and deduction. Some have difficulty identifying an instance of induction or deduction when it occurs. Others wonder if it's worthwhile to make a distinction in the first place. The situation is not helped when most material on teaching ignores the issue completely. Hopefully, the treatment which follows will be helpful.

The distinction between induction and deduction is worth making because there are significant implications for teaching. The case has been made for pluralism in teaching because of the increased availability of alternative strategies for teaching and questioning. That case applies here as well: Just as we are interested in eliciting a wide range of cognitive processes, we are concerned with providing a wide range of questioning strategies. Since the distinction between induction and deduction goes all the way back to the ancient Greeks, we would be slighting our students if we did not help them to appreciate the difference.

A lengthy philosophical treatise on the fine distinction between induction and deduction is beyond the scope of this chapter. It is sufficient to say that with induction we gather specific facts about events, people, objects, or places. We examine the particulars for connections. Then, from what we know to be true about the particulars, we form a general proposition. This general proposition may be a concept or a generalization which connects two or more concepts. The leap we make in coming to the concept or generalization is not a conclusion that is necessarily simple or obvious. Our minds go beyond the data and come up with something new that is not found in the data.

Some of the generalizations we form through induction are *conclusive* and some are *inconclusive*. For example, assume that we have gathered data about each of the fifty states in the United States of America with regard to location, temperature zones, agriculture, and population. We examine the particulars and form the generalization "No state in the U.S.A. reaches as far south as the equator." This is a *conclusive* generalization because we have examined every and all of the fifty particular cases. We know that there are only fifty states and we have dealt with the locations of all fifty of them.

On the other hand, we might formulate the following generalization based on our examination of the data: "People who live in cities along the Pacific Ocean live longer than people who live in cities along the Atlantic Ocean." This generalization, if it is true, is inconclusive because we haven't examined the population of every city along both coasts of the U.S.A., nor have we examined the population of cities along the coasts outside the U.S.A. In short, we haven't examined all the cases. It is possible that in the future we will find a particular case which negates our generalization. For this reason the generalization is *inconclusive*.

Below is a brief extract from an inductive questioning strategy dealing again with bicycles. Note the progression of questions.

Teacher: What data have you collected on the source of bikes in the U.S.?

Steve: I collected data on ten-speed bikes. According to Tony, who owns the bike store, the most popular bikes are the Japanese, English, American, and French, in that order. Far behind, he believes, are the Korean and Czech bikes—and he doesn't even sell those. He just reads about them in some bike magazine he gets.

Carol: I got the data on the regular one-speed bikes. Most of those bikes are American made but more and more are coming in from Europe and Asia.

Teacher: What else?

Mindy: I collected information on three-speed bikes. These were the old racing bikes until a few years ago when tens became popular. The most popular threes are still the English. The American manufacturers never really entered this market, so the English have always had it.

(The discussion continues with other people contributing further data and comments on those data.)

Teacher: Now let's look at all these facts about where our bikes come from. What conclusion do you reach about the bikes we ride?

Carol: It seems fair to say that our fancy bikes are foreign imports while our standard bikes are American.

In this extract it is clear that the teacher and students begin with the particulars of the case by gathering data on the different types of bicycles. Once the data are collected and discussed, the class draws a conclusion in the form of a general statement. They induce the generalization from the data before them. (Furthermore, it appears from this much of the interaction that the teacher is also utilizing a plateaus strategy.)

With deduction we begin with certain premises or facts which may or may not be true. From these premises or facts we draw a conclusion. Through a chain of statements, each of which is a premise or fact accepted previously, we come to conclusion. When we deduce a conclusion we come to a *conclusive* statement, one that must be so.

Our conclusive statement can be troublesome in two ways. First, our starting premises may be false and they may lead us to draw a valid but false conclusion. Thus there is a distinction to be made between the terms valid, which describes our process of reasoning, and truth, which describes the world as we observe it with our senses. Second, we can err in our deducing and therefore arrive at an invalid and false conclusion. To assess the conclusion we must be sure that our line of reasoning is correct *and* that our premises are true. If the reasoning is correct *and* the premises true, then our conclusion is also valid and true. In this way, the statement we make is conclusive.

Below is a brief extract from a deductive questioning strategy dealing again with bicycles. Note the progression of questions and the reasoning.

Teacher:	We talked about the parts of your bikes during the last lesson. Now I'd like you to consider the following statement and see what you can conclude from it. If a part of your bike comes with the bike from the factory, then that part has a positive purpose according to the designer. Would you please name some parts that come with your bikes and we'll see what we can say about them.
Mandy:	My handbrakes came with the bike.
George:	The fenders, the handlegrips, the tires.
Sue:	The pedals with reflectors.
Teacher:	O.K. That's great. Now what do you conclude about the brakes, fenders, handlebars.
George:	I said handle*grips*.
Teacher:	Thanks. Handlegrips, tires, and pedals?
Mandy:	That they all have positive purposes.
Phyllis:	My kickstand has a good purpose too 'cause without it I'd ruin my bike.

Teacher: What can you say based on Phyllis' statement?
George: That it came with her bike from the factory?
Phyllis: You can't say that, George, 'cause my bike didn't come with a kickstand. None of the Fuji S10S bikes do. I had to put it on myself at the bike store.
Teacher: Excellent. We can't conclude that about the kickstand, but what you concluded about the other parts is absolutely right.

Note here that the deduction about the handbrakes, fenders, handlegrips, tires, and pedals is valid and true. The deductive reasoning is valid. First comes the conditional premise, "If a part of your bike comes with the bike from the facory, then that part has a positive purpose according to the designer." Then comes the second premise, "My handbrakes (and the fenders, handlegrips, tires, and pedals) came with the bike." From these two premises it *is valid*[7] to deduce that these parts have a positive purpose. It is a conclusive conclusion.

The deduction that the kickstand came with the bike is invalid. (George's comment is not a question but a response, and Phyllis took it as a response. It is in interrogative form because it reflects George's uncertainty. Despite the inflected voice as shown in writing by the question mark, George's statement is a response.) It is invalid, as shown below in Type 2: Affirming the Consequent, to conclude from the conditional premise and the claim about the kickstand's positive purpose that the kickstand must have come with the bike from the factory.[8]

There are four basic forms of conditional reasoning. Below are brief examples of each of the four with a notation of whether that type is valid or invalid reasoning. Each starts with a *conditional premise* containing an *antecedent* and a *consequent*. Next comes a *second premise* affirming or denying one part of the conditional premise. Then comes a *conclusion*.

[7]For an excellent explanation of validity and logical reasoning see Robert H. Ennis, *Logic in Teaching* (Englewood Cliffs, N.J.: Prentice-Hall, Inc., 1969), pp. 13-63.
[8]Ibid.

Type 1: Affirming the Antecedent (Valid reasoning)
　　Cond. Prem.:　If Miami is in Florida, then Miami is in the U.S.A.
　　2nd Prem.:　Miami is in Florida
　　Conclusion:　Miami is in the U.S.A. (Valid)

Type 2: Affirming the Consequent (Invalid reasoning)
　　Cond. Prem.:　If Miami is in Florida, then Miami is in the U.S.A.
　　2nd Prem.:　Miami is in the U.S.A.
　　Conclusion:　Miami is in Florida (Invalid)

Type 3: Denying the Antecedent (Invalid reasoning)
　　Cond. Prem.:　If Miami is in Florida, then Miami is in the U.S.A.
　　2nd Prem.:　Miami is not in Florida
　　Conclusion:　Miami is not in the U.S.A. (Invalid)

Type 4: Denying the Consequent (Valid reasoning)
　　Cond. Prem.:　If Miami is in Florida, then Miami is in the U.S.A.
　　2nd Prem.:　Miami is not in the U.S.A.
　　Conclusion:　Miami is not in Florida (Valid)

Some people wish to contrast deduction and induction. This is appropriate if we restrict the meaning of the term induction to the inconclusive type of generalizing. Then we would have *inconclusive in contrast with conclusive* reasoning. If, however, we allow induction to include both inconclusive and conclusive conclusions, then it is inappropriate to contrast induction with deduction in this regard.

Inductive and deductive questioning strategies are both appropriate in teaching. The deductive strategy, however, requires that the respondents have mature cognitive abilities because there is more reliance on abstract reasoning. If it is a simple issue, you may judge that the students are able to deal with the topic deductively. According to Piaget, however, students need to be in the *formal stage* of development which begins around the age of eleven or twelve.[9] Thus, a deductive strategy may be inappropriate for students who have not reached the formal stage of development.

On the other hand, inductive strategies are appropriate once students have reached the *concrete stage* of cognitive development. According to Piaget, students reach the concrete stage at the age of seven or eight.[10] As before, it is up to you as teacher to judge each group of students separately to determine the students' ability to draw inductive conclusions from available data.

Practice Exercise 5
Inductive Strategy and Deductive Strategy

For this exercise refer to the preceding two extracts dealing with bicycles. See pages 50–52.

In regard to the inductive strategy keep in mind that one question asks the respondent to state specific facts on bicycles and one question asks the respondent to make a generalization based on the available data.

In regard to the deductive strategy keep in mind that the teacher offers a first premise which is a conditional premise, then the students name parts of their bikes, and then the students draw a conclusion.

Write your responses to each of the eight items below.

A. For the Inductive Strategy
  1. Suggest two questions eliciting causes, purposes, or se-

---

[9]John H. Flavell, *The Developmental Psychology of Jean Piaget* (Princeton: D. Van Nostrand Company, Inc., 1963), p. 86.
[10]Ibid.

quences of events that would be appropriate to insert between the two questions in the extract.

2. Suggest two questions eliciting consequences that would be appropriate between the two questions in the extract.

3. Suggest a question eliciting a consequence of a nonevent that would be appropriate between the two questions in the extract.

4. Suggest your own three- to five-step inductive strategy dealing with the topic "The Bikes We Ride."

B. For the Deductive Strategy

5. Suggest a valid conclusion of Phyllis' first comment had been "My seat cover doesn't help me out in any good way."

6. Suggest a valid conclusion if Phyllis' first comment had been "My basket didn't come with the bike."

7. Suggest an alternative first conditional premise the teacher could have used.

8. Suggest a possible three-step deductive strategy on the topic "The Bikes We Ride."

Author's Responses to Practice Exercise 5
Inductive Strategy and Deductive Strategy

1. a. Why are the Japanese bikes the leading ten-speed bikes?
   b. Compare and contrast the purposes served by the one-, three-, and ten-speed bikes.

2. a. If the Japanese bikes become the leading one-speed bikes, what effect will that have on U.S. industry?
   b. If the U.S. tries to capture the ten-speed bike market, what do you think will happen?

3. If Japan hadn't become the ten-speed leader, what would have happened to bikes a few years ago?

4. a. What kind of bike do you ride?
   b. How did it come about that you ride such a bike?
   c. Do you enjoy riding your bike?
   d. From what we've heard, what can you say about the bikes people in this group ride?

5. My seat cover didn't come with the bike. (See Ennis in footnote 7 at the end of the chapter.)

6.   There is no valid conclusion based on this statement and the existing first premise. It is invalid to conclude that "my basket has a positive function." (See Ennis in footnote 7 at the end of this chapter.)

7.   If the part on your bike is a moving part, then it is crucial to the bike.

8. **a.**   People enjoy riding fancy and fast bikes.

     b.   My bike is a deluxe ten-speed racer.

     c.   I enjoy riding my bike.

FIVE

FIFTEEN SPECIFIC QUESTIONING STRATEGIES

The previous chapter presented a set of five general strategies for questioning. This chapter presents a set of fifteen *specific* strategies whose goal is the performance of various cognitive tasks. None of the strategies is tied to a given topic or field of study. It would be possible, through reorganization and refinement, to expand the number of strategies. The purpose here, however, is not to overwhelm you as questioner but rather to provide a manageable set of basic strategies with which you may work as you teach. As you use these strategies you will naturally modify them to fit your particular approach to teaching and your specific subject matter. These strategies will become the basis for your questioning.

FORMAT AND PURPOSE

The format for each of the following strategies is the same. In the left-hand column are the questions you ask as a questioner. Sometimes there are questions in parentheses which are alternative phrasings of the questions. The questions are obviously listed in a particular sequence, the sequence being an essential part of the strategy. In the right-hand column there are descriptions of what the respondent does when answering the questions. This list will help you understand the reasons for the questions and see the progression of cognitive tasks which the respondents perform. It is absolutely necessary that your students, not you, respond to the questions as their way of processing the information they have. By responding to the questions the students commit themselves to the conclusions that they reach. Their stake in the conclusion makes the conclusion meaningful to them.

You can use a plateaus, peaks, or combined plateaus and peaks strategy (see Chapter 4) as you ask the students your questions. As presented here, for example, Strategy 1 lends itself to the plateaus strategy. With this general approach you will need to ask each question several times to various students before proceeding to the next of the nine steps in developing a concept. Nevertheless, it is certainly possible and acceptable to use a peaks strategy in developing a concept. It is also possible and acceptable to use a combined plateaus and peaks strategy. For example, you may use a plateaus strategy for question 1; then a series of peaks for questions 2, 3, and 4; and then a series of plateaus for questions 5 through 9. There is no absolute rule as to which general strategy to use. You will have to determine that for yourself.

As you proceed through each strategy you will have the opportunity to modify the questions. You can add response clues, change the information-process activity, and rephrase a question so as to form an alternative method of eliciting the same cognitive process. You will have this opportunity when using a plateaus approach or a series of peaks questions. You are free to modify—by rephrasing and/or adding supplementary questions—so as to create a variety of questions which you believe will work for you.

It is also possible to modify a strategy by switching from an inductive to a deductive approach. All but one of the specific strategies presented here are designed around an inductive approach since that is suitable to a wider range of students than the deductive approach. As an example of such a possibility, I shall demonstrate how you can modify Strategy 1 so that it will become a deductive method of developing concepts.

As you read these specific strategies you will notice a deemphasis on the question "Why?" which is commonly used by teachers.[1] The why question imposes pressure on respondents and requires them to defend themselves. It tends to create a tone which may run counter to your goal of involving the respondents in performing certain cognitive tasks publicly. This is especially true of why questions in the evaluative mode of thought. (For example, "Why do you support the President's energy plan?" and "Why do you value security more than freedom?"). There is also a definite threat when an empirical question deals with an action or event related to the respondent personally. (For example, "Why did you go swimming yesterday?") With other empirical matters, why questions are less threatening because they have no personal overtones. For example, "Why did it rain yesterday?" is not likely to be threatening unless the respondents have some conduct or experience which they associate with the question and which causes them some personal concern.

One group of educators specializing in affective education has gone so far as to suggest a moratorium on why questions.[2] I have not taken an absolute position because I have distinguished among various uses of the why question. I have used the why question a few times in the fifteen strategies but only in those situations where the respondent is to give a reason for a neutral, external situation. This is a deemphasis and not a

[1]Arno A. Bellack, Herbert M. Kleibard, Ronald T. Hyman, and Frank L. Smith, Jr., *The Language of the Classroom* (New York: Teachers College Press, 1966), p. 121.
[2]Mark R. Shedd, Norman A. Newberg, and Richard H. de Leone, "Yesterday's Curriculum—Today's World: Time to Reinvent the Wheel," in *The Curriculum: Retrospect and Prospect*, Seventieth Yearbook, Part I, of the National Society for the Study of Education, ed. Robert M. McClure (Chicago: The National Society for the Study of Education, 1971), pp. 153-80.

total elimination. To reduce the negative side effects of the why question I have relied on other questions which yield alternative ways of eliciting reason giving that I have found to be less threatening to students. Furthermore, by using the tactic of increased wait-time as well as other tactics, it is possible for students to offer reasons voluntarily and without threat. See Chapter 6 for questioning dialogues to learn these techniques.

In short, these specific strategies are to be viewed as foundations to build on. They may be modified by you to suit your students and subject area, and can be used in conjunction with the five general strategies presented earlier. The strategies should not be considered as rigid in terms of phrasing of the individual questions, and they shouldn't be viewed as the only ones you can or should use. In actual use you might never use the strategy exactly as presented in terms of the number of questions asked, the exact order, or the phrasing of the questions. What you have with each strategy is a keystone on which to construct a custom-built strategy.

These strategies show the influence of many other educators. The most obvious and important is Hilda Taba who deserves the praise of all questioning strategists for her research work at San Francisco State University.[3] With these general and introductory comments in mind, let us proceed to the specific strategies.

Strategy 1: Developing Concepts Inductively
(Categorizing, Classifying)

Questioner	Respondent
1. List what you observed.	1. Describe's the items.

[3]See Taba's research reports. Hilda Taba, Samuel Levine, and Freeman F. Elzey, *Thinking in Elementary School Children* (San Francisco: San Francisco State College, 1964); and Hilda Taba, *Teaching Strategies and Cognitive Functioning in Elementary School Children* (San Francisco: San Francisco State College, 1966). Her associates continued her work after her untimely death.

(Report about what you saw/tasted/smelled/heard/read.)

2. What items (events, factors) go together?	2. Groups items.
3. So far what is the common thread among these items?	3. Gives common factor among items for grouping.
4. What do you call each of the various groups which you have formed?	4. Labels the groups.
5. Are these groups distinct— that is, do the items belong to one group only?	5. Examines groupings.
6. If there are overlaps, which items belong to more than one group?	6. Identifies complexity in the groupings.
7. Suggest, if possible, a whole other way to group these items and/or label them.	7. Offers alternatives.
8. What is the common thread among these items for grouping and/or labeling this alternative way?	8. Gives common factor for new grouping and/or labeling.
9. In light of these groupings, what categories (concepts, labels) do we now have?	9. Summarizes by giving final groupings.

Strategy 1 focuses on developing concepts, which are the building blocks for forming generalizations. We form concepts as our way of coping with the multitudes of specific facts that we encounter daily. Concepts are ideas which we label so as to represent what is common to many individual items or experiences. Concepts offer us a way of simplifying as well as understanding the world around us. For this reason they are extremely important, and therefore the strategies for developing them deserve significant attention.

Strategy 1 builds upon an observation activity. This activity may be one that you have prepared for your students or one that has occurred spontaneously. The activity may be a viewing, tasting, hearing, touching, reading, or a combination of these activities. After the students have had an opportunity to observe, you begin your questioning so as to guide them in developing a concept inductively. Let us assume that you wish to introduce the concept of "democratic government." You might ask various students to read about the following governments in their texts, encyclopedias, or other library references: ancient Egypt, Nazi Germany, Saudi Arabia, Mexico, England, France, modern Japan, Canada, Italy, Brazil, and Lebanon. Or you might wish to show a film or film strip on these or other governments. You may wish to lecture, giving information about the governments of selected past and present countries. Once the students have the information, you may begin the questioning strategy.

No matter what the activity is that provides the foundation of information, the key elements for this strategy as well as all the others will be the series of questions which you ask and the responses which the students themselves offer. The responses of the students constitute the cognitive processes which develop the concept. That is, the *students* must group the various governments (step 2), examine the groups (step 5), offer alternative groupings (step 7), and give final labels and groupings (step 9). In this way the students process the information themselves and come to see the possible relationships among the governments. When they perform these processes, they have a strong stake in the concept being developed. They have, so to speak, ownership of the concept because they have manipulated the data by grouping the various governments, labeling the groups, regrouping, defending their suggested groupings, and establishing final groupings.

It is important for the students to note that it is often possible to categorize an item into more than one group. It is difficult to establish completely discrete groups even in such subject areas as language and mathematics (symbol systems), and it is even more difficult in the humanities and social sciences. Furthermore, concepts and categories reflect our own way of structuring the world. They are not inherent in events and situations.

It is important, therefore, that you pay careful attention to steps 5, 6, and 7 of this strategy. You should ask for and accept many suggestions of ways in which the various governments overlap. You should also elicit different ways of grouping the governments according to varying points of view.

Strategy 2: Developing Concepts Deductively
(Categorizing, Classifying)

Questioner	Respondent
1. This grouping of items (events, factors) is called———.	
2. What is the basis for grouping the items in this way?	2. Gives reason for grouping; gives common thread among items.
3. Given this basis, what additional items clearly fit into this group?	3. Lists additional items that fit the concept; applies concept to specific items to include them.
4. Given this basis, what related items clearly do not fit into this group?	4. Lists other items that do not fit the concept; applies concept to specific items to exclude them.
5. Given this basis, what related items are borderline members of this group?	5. Lists other items that partially fit the concept; applies concept to specific items to note unclear cases.
6. In light of these items which fit and do not fit the concept, state the key characteristics of this group. (Restate the definition of the concept.)	6. Summarizes by giving a conclusion based on applying the concept (category; class) to specific items.

Strategy 2 is a deductive approach to developing concepts. It appears here as one example of modifying available inductive questioning strategies, which are more common and applicable to all age levels of students. According to Morine and Morine the deductive strategies are "useful with children who are in the formal operations stages, ages eleven or twelve and beyond. We do not believe that these . . . lessons can be taught very effectively to many elementary children . . . ."[4] The limitation on the use of a deductive strategy does not imply in any way that you should never employ Strategy 2 or another deductive one. Rather, you must carefully consider your students' ability to respond within a deductive strategy.

With Strategy 2 you begin your questioning only after you present the concept as applied to a selected number of cases. Let's return to the previous example about democratic governments. You could describe several governments (for example, those of Canada, France, Israel, and Austria), which you would group together and label as democratic. After you had introduced the concept, you would begin your questioning. The student's role would be to respond to your questions, which would elicit application of the concept to further specific governments. When the students had dealt with further specific governments (for example, those of Saudi Arabia, Nazi Germany, modern Japan, Mexico, ancient Egypt), they could restate the concept as their way of showing that they had meaningfully developed the concept of a democratic government.

It is important to note that the students themselves must apply the concept to further specific governments. They need to list the governments that fit the concept of democracy as well as listing the governments that do not fit. Listing only those that fit or only those that do not fit will not suffice. The students themselves must likewise make the concluding

---

[4]Harold Morine and Greta Morine, *Discovery: A Challenge to Teachers* (Englewood Cliffs, N.J.: Prentice-Hall, Inc., 1973), p. 97.

statement, for it provides proof that they have grasped the concept.

Practice Exercise 6
(Refer to Strategies 1 and 2.)

1. Briefly describe an activity in which you would involve your young, elementary school students as a foundation for developing inductively the concepts of evergreen trees or triangles.
2. Suppose that you will lead a group of junior high school students to develop deductively the concept of free verse in poetry. Describe in general what items you would present to them as examples. Give the general statement that would serve as the organizing device (see step 2 of Strategy 2) for this strategy.

Strategy 3: Comparing and Contrasting

Questioner	Respondent
1. Precisely describe each of the events (people, objects).	1. Identifies and describes the items as basis for comparing and contrasting.
2. Which elements in the events are the key ones?	2. Selects essential parts of each event.
3. In what ways are the key elements of one event similar to and different from those of the other event?	3. Compares and contrasts with a focus on the essential elements.
4. What are the causes or effects of the similarities?	4. Gives reasons, explanations for similarities.
5. What are the causes or effects of the differences?	5. Gives reasons, explanations for differences.

6. In what ways are the minor elements of one event similar to and different from those of the other event?	6. Compares and contrasts with a focus on the minor elements.
7. What are the causes or effects of the similarities?	7. Gives reasons, explanations for similarities.
8. What are the causes or effects of the differences?	8. Gives reasons, explanations for differences.
9. What is the significance of all these similarities and differences, that is, what does this all mean?	9. Offers conclusions about the event.

Strategy 3 is an analytical one for comparing and contrasting events, situations, people, ideas, or objects. The first step is an eliciting of a precise, adequate, and accurate description of the items to be compared and contrasted. It may be necessary to repeat the first question several times, rephrasing it or adding the question "What else?" Once the descriptions are available for all of the respondents to draw upon, it is necessary to identify the key elements for each item so as to insure that the comparison/contrast is well balanced. If not, key elements of one item may be compared with minor elements of another item, resulting in a skewed comparison.

The emphasis in the comparison/contrast should be on the identified key elements. You should not ignore the minor elements, however, for they may yield the only differences among apparently similar items. Moreover, what is major and what is minor is not always absolutely clear. For example, if you are comparing/contrasting the tennis play of Ken Rosewall, Jimmy Connors, Bjorn Borg, and Rod Laver, you must consider such factors as age, strength of serve, type of backhand (one-hand or two-hand), and handedness (left-handed or right-handed). Though the respondents may not consider handedness as a key element, it is still worthwhile to consider the effect a left-handed player has with topspin and curve when playing against a right-handed player.

Once the respondents have offered comparisons, contrasts, causes, and effects, it is their task to draw conclusions. Their role is to decide what all the data mean. Since such a conclusion is based on an interpretation of the data, not all respondents may agree. Hence, it may be necessary to repeat the conclusion-eliciting question to different respondents. A difference in conclusions may lead you to return to steps 3–5 to reconsider and clarify matters.

Strategy 4: Analyzing a Document
(Story, Event)

Questioner	*Respondent*
1. From what perspective will you examine the document (story, event)? (What framework shall you use in your analysis?)	1. States viewpoint (framework, vantage point) to be used.
2. What are the advantages of using this perspective?	2. Gives reasons for using this viewpoint.
3. What are the essential features of this document from this perspective?	3. Identifies and describes the features.
4. From this perspective, in what ways is this document similar to or different from another familiar document?	4. Offers analogy for comparisons and contrast.
5. Are there any elements missing from the document that you'd expect to find since they are crucial to this perspective? If so, what are they?	5. Based on related documents, identifies what gaps there are.

6. What do these elements mean to you?	6. Offers importance and meaning of the identified elements.
7. What do you conclude about this document?	7. Offers conclusion about the document.
8. Repeat steps 1–7 but from another perspective.	8. Analyzes the document from a different perspective to gain further insight.
9. What do you conclude about this document based on the points arising from the various perspectives taken?	9. Synthesizes the many points raised and offers a multi-faceted conclusion.

Strategy 4 is also an analytical one. This strategy focuses on one document, story, essay, or event as is frequently done in subjects such as literature, history, and biology. The key to this strategy, as with any analysis or observation, is the perspective taken. The perspective, framework, or vantage point determines the concepts to be applied to the document. The analysis, therefore, directly reflects the perspective. For example, if you analyze George Orwell's novel *Animal Farm* from a Marxist perspective, the results will differ significantly from those obtained by using a Freudian or Machiavellian perspective. For this reason it is first necessary to clarify which perspective will be used in the analysis. Without such a clarification a discussion of the document will proceed with significant gaps in understanding among the students and teacher.

Once the perspective is identified, clarified, and justified in terms of the advantages offered by a particular perspective, the specific analysis can begin. The respondents identify and describe the important elements of the document as seen from the selected perspective. They compare the document with other documents based on what they do and do not find in the document.

To show the importance and effect of the perspective on

the analysis, you repeat steps 1–7 once or several times, gaining new insights each time. The final step is the question which elicits an overall conclusion based on all the perspectives taken. If time is at a premium, it is possible to stop at step 7 and continue with another perspective at a later date.

Strategy 5: Generalizing from Observation
or Experience (Developing or Forming
Generalization)

Questioner	*Respondent*
1. What happened? (What did you observe?)	1. Describes the event; gives data.
2. What else happened? (What else did you observe?)	2. Describes the event; gives data.
3. Continues to elicit information so as to build firm foundation of data.	3. Describes the event; gives data.
4. What are the similarities and differences among the events?	4. Compares and contrasts events.
5. Why did these events occur? (Or, How did these events occur?)*	5. Infers reasons for the events.
6. (If more than one person is involved or offers data and explanations, the questioner asks): Why (or how) did these events occur, according to persons A and B?*	6. Infers explanations from alternative viewpoint.
7. Describe a parallel situation which may give	7. Describes similar event for analogy.

*See other strategies on explanation regarding the differences between causal and sequential explanations.

us insight into these events
(situations).

8. What does all of this add up to? (What generalization can you offer based on these data? What's your conclusion?)	8. Develops generalization which connects the separate points into one overall statement.

Strategy 5 is similar to the two previous strategies in that the respondent draws a conclusion as the final step. Strategy 5 is different in that it focuses on eliciting much data, explaining that data, and establishing an acceptable generalization based on that data. Since the main goal is to generalize validly, it is necessary to elicit a firm foundation of data. Generalizations based on too little data often prove to be unacceptable at a later date. It is therefore possible to generalize only after plentiful data are available and considered.

After the data are elicited, the respondents need to work with them. The respondents compare and contrast and then explain the data. You may choose between a causal explanation (why did the events occur?) or a sequential (chronological) explanation (how did the events occur?) For the differences between these types of explanations see Strategies 8 and 10. (Refer to Chapter 2 under the section on empirical questions for a brief discussion of these different types of explanatory questions.)

To shed further light on the events, the respondents seek appropriate analogies. By offering analogies the respondents show that they understand the events in their context and at the same time come to see the events more clearly. Seeking and offering is a powerful springboard for the final step of generalizing. The offering of a generalization caps the strategy. As with previous strategies it is essential that the respondents themselves draw the final conclusion. The act of generalizing requires them to deal with the many events in a connected way. The respondent seeks connectedness and universality rather than separateness and specificity. Once formulated, the generalization becomes the stepping stone for predicting, which is one type of application and the goal of the next strategy.

Strategy 6: Predicting
(Applying Generalizations)

Questioner	Respondent
1. What precisely is the situation we're concerned with—its features and conditions?	1. Describes situation.
2. Given that this situation exists or will exist, what do you think will happen as a result? (What are the probable consequences of this situation?)	2. Predicts new situation or event.
3. What facts and generalizations support your prediction?	3. Supports prediction by applying a generalization and related facts.
4. What other things might happen as a result of this situation?	4. Offers alternative prediction.
5. If the predicted situation occurs, what will happen next?	5. Gives consequences of prediction.
6. In summary, what will lead us from the current situation to your predicted one?	6. Summarizes by showing connection fundamental to the prediction.

Strategy 6 focuses on the future by predicting what will happen as a result of an event or situation either now or in the future. In other words, "Given A, predict B." There are two bases of the strategy: A description of the situation is given, followed by a generalization that leads the predictor to move from the situation to the prediction. A precise description of the situation by the predictors allows everyone to recognize how the situation appears to those people. The predictors, in describing the situation, identify what is essential and important to them.

After the respondents describe, they predict what will happen as a result of the situation. Then they support the prediction with pertinent facts and the generalizations previously reached. Without this key step, the prediction is not a valid one but rather an unjustified or irrational guess. This step serves the functions of requiring respondents to think rationally regarding probable consequences of a situation and of reinforcing prior learning by asking the respondents to draw upon it. When students recognize that they will indeed be predicting and therefore applying generations, there is reason and motivation for developing valid and usable generalizations in the first place. The act of predicting offers the opportunity to apply previous cognitive achievements.

When the situation involves people and/or objects in the world, it is not possible to predict with 100 percent accuracy what will happen in the future. Due to the complexity of our world, it is not possible to identify and account for the interaction of all the many factors even in what may appear to be a simple situation. For this reason the next step of this predicting strategy is necessary: Offer an alternative prediction. This step serves to drive home the point that situations are multifaceted. Since it is possible to view situations differently, it is possible to predict that different results will occur. An awareness of alternative predictions serves as a reminder that any given prediction is but one possibility among many and therefore may turn out to be incorrect.

Practice Exercise 7
(Refer to strategies 3, 4, 5, and 6.)

1. Suppose you wish to have your students compare the 1960 election of President Kennedy and the 1976 election of President

Carter. Prepare two specific questions about these two Presidents which will help the students identify and clarify the major factors in these two events.

2. Suppose you wish to have your students in a literature class analyze Golding's *Lord of the Flies*. State at least two perspectives you could use in your analysis.

3. Suppose that you took a group of students on a field trip to a zoo. You visited the monkey section five minutes before feeding time. All of you saw the monkeys stretching out their arms toward the students who were eating some popcorn at the time. As a substitute for step 7 in Strategy 5, what two parallel situations might you ask the students to consider so as to gain insight into the monkey's behavior? That is, "How is the monkey's behavior similar to———?"

4. Suppose you wish to have your students consider the energy crisis now facing the world. Your students predict that due to a shortage of oil, the balance of power among nations will shift by the year 1995. They also predict that people will have to depend more on solar energy beginning now. What other two predicted situations would you add (your own contribution in step 4 of Strategy 6) so that your students could respond to them in step 5?

Strategy 7: Explaining How to Do Something

Questioner	*Respondent*
1. What is the first step in this procedure? (Demonstrate it if you can.)	1. Begins by stating and demonstrating the first step.
2. What are the remaining steps, one by one in order? Show them as you talk if you can.	2. Lists other steps in order and demonstrates.
3. Are there steps that you now want to add or omit?	3. Reflects on entire procedure to see if all is correct.

4. Must these steps be in the order you gave or can there be another order?	4. Reflects about correctness of order and alternatives.
5. If there is an alternative, what is this other possible order?	5. Gives alternative order.
6. What is the reason for the order you gave, that is, why must step 1 come before step 2, and so forth?	6. Gives reasons for the sequence of steps.
7. Give some suggestions and/or warnings (cautions) about this procedure.	7. Offers tips on how to do it correctly, easily, and safely.
8. About how much time, and/or space, and/or money is needed to complete this procedure?	8. Sets limits for the procedure.
9. To what other procedure is this similar?	9. Offers analogy for clarification.
10. Briefly summarize the key points of the whole procedure.	10. Reviews the entire sequence to tie it together.

Strategy 7 focuses on explaining to the questioner or someone else how to do something such as fix a flat tire, light a Bunsen burner, do a cartwheel, build a bookcase, weave a rug, dance the Virginia reel, or take a square root. The strategy requires the respondents to state the order of the procedure they are explaining. If at all possible the questioner should arrange for the respondents to actually demonstrate the activity as they describe the various steps involved. The oral explication and nonverbal demonstration complement each other.

Once the respondents state and demonstrate the steps, they then begin to reflect on the entire procedure. First they add or subtract steps if necessary. Then they consider the order of the steps. Perhaps the order they have given is not the best. Perhaps an alternative order can be found. This leads to a consideration of the reasons for the order as demonstrated or suggested. Then the respondents comment on considerations of time, space, money, and any other important factors of the procedure.

The questioner, just before concluding this strategy by requesting a complete review, asks the respondents to seek an analogy with another familiar procedure. This offering of an analogy as a parallel situation, as in previous strategies, serves to bring clarification to the explanation being offered. The respondents have the opportunity to add with their analogy any final details that will help explain how to do the procedure.

Strategy 8:
Explaining the Cause of an Event or Condition
by Showing that a Generalization Includes this
Specific Instance

Questioner		Respondent	
1.	What precisely is the event (condition, action, item) that needs to be explained?	1.	Identifies and describes the event.
2.	State a generalization (rule, law, norm) which is closely related to this event.	2.	States the generalization which will subsume the specific event to be explained
3.	What support do you have that this generalization is true (valid)?	3.	Establishes truth and acceptability of the generalization.
4.	What facts that we know about this event connect it with the generalization?	4.	Offers connecting evidence between event and generalization.
5.	Clarify that the connecting facts show the event to be a specific instance of the generalization.	5.	Demonstrates the generalization.

6.	Form a conclusion as to why the event occurred.	6.	Ties it all together to form a succinct explanation.

Strategy 8 also focuses on explaining. This strategy leads to an explanation of what caused a particular event or why a given condition or situation exists. This strategy offers an answer not to "how" but to "why." It answers the question "why" by showing that the particular instance under consideration is included in a generalization which is valid. For the other types of explanation, chronological and functional, see Strategies 9 and 10.

The first step in the strategy, as usual, is the precise description of the event under consideration. This makes it clear to everyone involved just what it is that needs to be explained. Next the respondents propose the generalization which subsumes the specific instance just described and show that it is true or valid and acceptable. For example, let us ask the question "Why is the attic hot today?" First the respondents identify that what they need to explain is the hot attic. Next they state a generalization which appears appropriate to subsume a specific attic being hot. They may offer the general statement that in a house the hot air rises to the top and remains there if it cannot escape. What is left to do is to fill the gap between the specific instance and the generalization.[5]

The respondents fill the gap by stating facts which connect the specific instance to the generalization. For example, they may state that today, August 20, the temperature is 98°F outside, a bright sun is shining down on the roof, the attic windows and vents are closed, and the attic temperature is 110°F. The gap-filling shows that the generalization is appropriate to this situation. If, on the other hand, the respondents cannot fill the gap, then it may well be that the generalization is not appropriate or does not subsume the specific instance.

Once the gap is filled, the respondents conclude by mak-

---

[5]Robert H. Ennis, *Logic in Teaching* (Englewood Cliffs, N.J.: Prentice-Hall, Inc., 1969), pp. 267-79.

ing a summary statement which is the overall answer to the question "Why did the event occur?" The attic is hot today because the hot air of the day has risen into the attic where it remains under the hot roof, unable to escape outside through the windows or vents.

Strategy 9:
Explaining a Situation by Showing Its Function
or Purpose

Questioner	Respondent
1. What precisely is the situation (person, action, object) that needs to be explained?	1. Identifies and describes the situation.
2. What is the function (purpose, intention) involved?	2. Identifies and describes or infers the function.
3. What facts do we have about this situation which connects it to the function?	3. Describes actions, people, and objects involved with the function.
4. Clarify that the situation fits the purpose; that the situation, person, action, or object carries out the function or achieves the purpose.	4. Demonstrates relationship between action and function.
5. State your conclusion from these points—that is, what is the reason for the condition?	5. Draws conclusion and ties all parts of the explanation together.

Strategy 9 focuses on explaining a situation or action by showing that the situation or action serves a particular function or purpose. This strategy, like Strategy 8, answers a "why" question. But here it is not a question of why the situation has occurred (what the causes are), but rather why the situation exists. For example, we may wish to know why car tires are made with nylon and steel, or why President Gerald Ford pardoned Richard Nixon, or why plants need water, or why humans have toes, or why tragedies have humorous sections in them, or why Rutgers University has its own legal staff.

Once again the first step in the explanation is the clear identification and description of the situation, action, or decision that needs to be explained. Next the respondents offer a statement of a function or purpose which is related to the situation. For example, you may ask why a university like Rutgers has its own legal staff. First, the respondents must identify the Rutgers staff lawyers and/or describe the position of "university lawyer" in the organizational structure of Rutgers. Next, the respondents offer a statement of the function of a lawyer in a large state university (or any large corporation such as Prentice-Hall, Inc., publisher of this book). The statement may be that a lawyer is needed who intimately knows the law and who can continually advise Rutgers about legal matters which persistently appear, such as negotiating with labor organizations representing the employees and interpreting federal laws regarding affirmative action hiring of minorities.

What remains for the respondents to show is that the Rutgers lawyers respond continually to the requests of the university's staff, the court, the federal government, and the state government regarding Rutgers' position on legal matters. By showing, for example, that the Rutgers lawyers inspect contracts with the various labor organiztions to be sure that they comply with state and federal regulations regarding discrimination, the respondents show that it is financially cheaper and more efficient for Rutgers to have its own devoted legal staff available for consultation than it is to hire private lawyers on retainer.

The concluding response ties all the statements together

to answer the question "why." The conclusion is an explanation in terms of function or purpose performed rather than in terms of what caused the situation. The questioner must be clear from the outset that an explanation of function is what is desired rather than an explanation of cause. If not, the respondents may not respond as expected, since the causal explanation is more common. From the form of the original question it is often not possible to know what is expected. For example, from the question "What is the reason Rutgers has its own legal staff?" it is possible to launch into a causal explanation based on financial savings; or a functional explanation based on availability of services and intimacy of knowledge of the issues.

Strategy 10:
Explaining the Cause of an Event by Showing
the Events Which Led Up to It

Questioner	Respondent
1. What precisely is the event (action, condition) that needs to be explained? We'll call this "Event E" to stand for Event to be Explained.	1. Identifies and describes Event E, the event to be explained.
2. What led to Event E?	2. Identifies Event 1, the event preceding Event E.
3. We'll call this preceding event "Event 1." What led to Event 1?	3. Identifies Event 2, the event preceding Event 1.
4. What led to Event 2?	4. Identifies Event 3, the event preceding Event 2.
5. Continue this process as far back and in as much detail as needed to satisfy	5. Identifies the series of events.

the Questioner and
Respondent*

	the Questioner and Respondent*		
6.	State your conclusion about what caused Event E. (Give a summary of the series of events leading to it.)	6.	Summarizes and concludes about the series of Events (Event 3→Event 2→Event 1→Event E).

*You may have to insert or solicit something between Event E and Event 1, Event 1 and Event 2, Event 2 and Event 3, etc., if someone doesn't understand how one event leads to the other. Or, if you see a gap somewhere in a response and you want more detail and precision, you may have to insert or elicit more specific events to complete the series.

Strategy 10 is the fourth and last strategy dealing with explanation. This strategy focuses on explaining why an event happened in terms of the series of events which led up to that event. The explanation thus consists of enumerating the events in a continuous sequence so that the preceding necessary and relevant events result in the event to be explained, Event E.

As before, the first step is the identification and description of the event to be explained. The next step begins the enumeration of the sequence preceding Event E. The respondents identify Event 1, the event which led to Event E. Then they identify Event 2, the event which led to Event 1 which led to Event E. This backward process continues until the questioner and respondents are satisfied that they know why Event E happened. For example, suppose you wish to explain the death (Event E) of John Jones yesterday afternoon. You can say that a car accident (Event 1) led to his death; a flat tire while driving at 70 m.p.h. (Event 2) led to the crash; and driving with a faulty and bald tire (Event 3) led to the flat tire.

Obviously, with this type of explanation there is no way to determine ahead of time just how far back it is necessary to go in order to satisfy the questioner and respondents. Someone can always ask "But what led to the event?" after each new event is identified. In the example above someone can ask "What led John Jones to drive with a faulty and bald tire?"

Thus, if someone fails to understand and be satisfied, it is possible to continue identifying preceding events until someone else demands a halt out of boredom, frustration, or anger.

As questioner you must be careful to check on understanding so that the backward enumeration process does not continue longer than necessary. You can often increase understanding by soliciting the respondents to fill in gaps between two events with more specific information and/or events.[6] In the example above, it is possible to show that the car crash (Event 1) led to being thrown out of the car which led to a head injury which led to an internal hemorrhage, which led to death (Event E). By filling in gaps between events, a dissatisfied person can achieve understanding and hence satisfaction. In this way you need not continually push for additional events further back in the sequence since you have added information between two already stated events.

As usual, in the final step the respondents summarize all the events mentioned in the series so that the series of events leading up to the event under consideration is clear. This summary constitutes an explanation and an answer to the question "How did Event E come about?" or "Why did Event E occur?" or "What caused Event E?"

Practice Exercise 8
(Refer to Strategies 7, 8, 9, and 10)

1. Suggest a skill in each of the following areas which you could ask your students to explain: physical science, art, dance, biology, geography, and home economics.
2. Suppose your students are explaining the cause of a traffic jam on the freeway between Los Angeles and Pasadena. Suppose that in step 2 of Strategy 8 they offer this generalization:

[6]Jane Roland Martin, *Explaining, Understanding, and Teaching* (New York: McGraw-Hill Book Co., 1970), pp. 37-59.

Whenever there is a football game or a hot, sunny weekend, the freeway is overloaded. Suggest some specific facts you would accept from your students as connecting evidence in step 4.

3. Suggest a person in government, an animal in the forest ecology, and the rules of some popular sport which your students could explain by showing their function or purpose.

4. Suppose your students are explaining the resignation of Richard Nixon as President. One student states "Watergate led to his resignation." What three specific events between the resignation (Event E) and the Watergate break-in (Event 1) could you insert or solicit to clarify this explanation?

Strategy 11: Analyzing Values
(Someone Else's or Your Own)

Questioner	Respondent
1. What is the value that person X expresses?	1. Identifies the value.
2. What does person X do that is connected with this value?	2. States behavior which manifests this value. This may be behavior explicitly identified as such by person X or behavior identified by the respondents.
3. Why does person X do these things?	3. States reasons for the behavior. These may be reasons explicitly expressed by person X or reasons inferred from behavior identified above.
4. How does person X feel about all of this?	4. States feelings related to this value. These may be feelings explicitly expressed by person X or inferred from X's behavior.

5. What do these actions, reasons, and feelings tell you about person X?
6. Describe a parallel situation that you know about concerning another person or yourself.
7. What does this parallel situation tell you about the person involved?
8. What differences are there between person X and this other person?
9. What similarities are there between person X and this other person?
10. What do you conclude about person X and this value?

5. States what is important (what is significant) to person X.
6. Describes a parallel situation for comparison and further probing.
7. States what is important to this other person.
8. Contrasts the two people or situations to sharpen analysis.
9. Compares the two people or situations to sharpen analysis.
10. Draws conclusion about person X and the value.

Strategy 11 is the first of four strategies that focus on values and feelings. The previous strategies have focused on conceptual and empirical matters though it is surely possible to adapt them easily to apply to affective matters. It is possible, for example, to adapt strategies 3 (comparing and contrasting) and 5 (generalizing) to apply to values. Strategies 11–14 focus specifically on values and feelings, for values and feelings are an integral part of teaching whether or not they are explicitly recognized.

The first step in this strategy for analyzing values is to identify the value under consideration and to connect it with some particular person or group of people. Values do not exist in the world apart from the minds of people. Once the respondents identify the value, either someone else's or their own, they then identify the behavior which manifests this value. They must connect the value with behavior since we do not and cannot deal with values directly. People have values and express them through their behavior. If you wish to analyze freedom as a value, you must connect it with Jane Doe's behavior and not just her statements about equality. What Jane Doe says about equality is important to consider, but you must also examine her behavior connected with equality since it may lead to a somewhat different view of equality.

Next, the respondents examine the reasons for this value and the feelings connected with it. Because of the nature of values it is important to know why people hold the values they do and how they feel about them. How do people justify their values? Do they feel proud about their values? Do they feel guilty? Do they feel defensive? Just what specific feelings do they have? Sometimes the respondents can report the reasons and feelings explicitly expressed by the people involved. Sometimes the respondents will have to infer reasons and feelings from the behavior which they have already identified. Moreover, even when they can report reasons and feelings for clarity the respondents may need to add to their analysis by inferring reasons and feelings on their own.

For example, let us assume that you are analyzing Jane Doe's value of equality. You may state that Jane Doe says that she believes in equality between the sexes and you may supply a reason pointed out by Jane Doe herself as justifying her value. But in addition to stating her reason as legitimate (she believes in equality because without it the U.S.A. cannot achieve continued economic superiority), you may want to add a reason which you infer from your knowledge of Jane Doe. You may state that her belief in equality stems from her religious conviction of equality for all people on Earth. From these inferences you can now supply three reasons for her value; one economic, one religious, and one related to her upbringing.

To further the analysis of the value the respondents next seek a parallel solution. Parallels serve the same purpose with value issues as they do with empirical ones. They are a useful and powerful step leading to clarity. The respondents finish this strategy drawing a conclusion from all the identified behavior, reasons, feelings, and parallels. This conclusion is a statement leading to an understanding of the value under consideration and not necessarily a commitment to that value. The following three strategies focus on commitment and clarification of values.

*Strategy 12: Clarifying Feelings or Attitudes
(Someone Else's or Your Own)*

Questioner	*Respondent*
1. What happened to person X?	1. Describe the situation.
2. How does person X feel about this?	2. States feelings. These may be feelings explicitly expressed by person X or inferred from X's behavior.
3. Are person X's feelings (attitude) appropriate to this situation?	3. Assesses feelings in relation to situation.
4. What led person X to feel this way?	4. Offers an explanation for the feeling expressed by person X.
5. Describe a similar situation that happened to you.	5. Offers a parallel situation for comparison of situations.
6. How did you feel in that situation?	6. Describes and explains feelings in similar situation.
7. Describe now a situation where you had a similar feeling as person X.	7. Describes and explains similar feelings in another situation (this complements first analogy for added insight).
8. What does all this tell you about person X's feelings?	8. Summarizes the clarification by drawing a conclusion.

Strategy 12 focuses on the clarification of feelings or attitude. The aim of the strategy is to allow and encourage the respondents to reflect upon feelings or attitudes, an area often neglected in the classroom. If the feelings are someone else's rather than the respondent's own feelings, then the strategy leads to developing empathy with that person. Whereas the previous strategy focuses on values, this strategy focuses on feelings which people have. The difference in strategies stems from the difference between values, ideas, or concepts, for which the phrase "I believe this is important or worthwhile" is appropriate, and feelings or attitudes which relate to a person's physical sensations or emotional disposition. Values are more cognitive whereas feelings are more physical and emotional.

To clarify feelings the respondents first describe the situation connected with the feeling and the feelings related to that situation. If the *situation* is of main importance, then the order of questions is as given here. If the *feelings* are the center of attention, then the order given here should be reversed. It is up to you as questioner to decide which question to ask first.

Next the respondents make an assessment about the appropriateness of the feelings in relation to the situation. They may claim that the feeling expressed constitutes an inappropriate reaction, an overreaction, or an appropriate reaction to the situation which occurred. Then the respondents explain what led the person involved (themselves or another person) to have those feelings. Note that the explanation requested is a chronological or sequential one (Strategy 10) rather than one which requests a justification in terms of general principles or purpose. This is done to avoid defensiveness on the part of the respondents, especially if they are clarifying their own feelings. The chronological or sequential explanation removes much of the personal threat posed by a why question seeking justification of feelings expressed.

For further clarification the respondents use the familiar technique of seeking parallels. They seek two parallels, the first of which focuses on a parallel situation which may have elicited similar or different feelings. The second parallel focuses on feelings which may or may not have stemmed from a similar situation. The two parallels complement each other so as to yield insight into the feelings being clarified. To end the clarifying process the respondents summarize the points raised by drawing a conclusion about the feeling expressed by someone else or themselves.

Strategy 13: Resolving Value Conflicts
(Someone Else's or Your Own)

Questioner	Respondent
1. What is the value conflict about?	1. Identifies and describes the conflict.
2. What are the key words used in talking about this conflict?	2. Identifies central concepts.
3. Define the key terms.	3. Defines essential terms for clarity of communication.
4. What are the possible actions open to person X that will resolve the conflict? (What can person X do?)	4. Describe alternatives available.
5. What are the likely consequences if person X took the first (second, third, etc.) alternative?	5. Predicts consequences of the various alternatives.
6. What are the chances that these consequences will occur?	6. Estimates likelihood of consequences happening.
7. Which consequences are good (desirable, preferred, advantageous) and which are not good?	7. Evaluates the consequences.

8.	What is or would be a similar, related conflict and its resolution?	8.	Describes a parallel situation.
9.	Is there a general principle which indicates which value has priority over the other? If so, what is it?	9.	Seeks overall ranking of values which will subsume this particular instance of conflict.
10.	At this point, what do you think person X should do to resolve the conflict?	10.	Expresses resolution based on previous points.
11.	What are the reasons for resolving the conflict this way?	11.	Gives reasons, justifies the suggested resolution to the value conflict.

Strategy 13 focuses on the resolution of value conflict. Conflict occurs to everyone because dearly held values often appear in a situation where the person involved must choose between equally important values. For example, you may believe strongly in equality and liberty. However, when officials call for compulsory busing of students (a one-hour trip) from one city to the next to achieve racial integration and balance, you may find yourself caught in a value conflict between equality and liberty, both of which you see as important to you. On the one hand you approve of busing, and on the other hand you do not.

The first step, though it appears simple, requires careful consideration. The respondents must identify and describe the conflict at hand. Often the respondents take a while before being able to pinpoint just where the conflict resides. It is essential that as questioner you seek several responses to this question. If you sense difficulty in identifying the conflict, you may proceed to the next two steps concerning the key terms and then return to the identification of the conflict. Once the key terms are made known it may be easier to decide just what the conflict is.

Because people are tense due to conflict, especially if it's their own conflict, it is necessary to be sure that clear communication occurs. The respondents must accept common definitions of key terms in order to talk about the issue. Using the example of busing, if people have a different definition of such terms as equality, liberty, self-determination, safety, and inconvenience, they will have a difficult time resolving the conflict as they see it.

Next, the respondents must enumerate the possible actions available to the person in conflict. This too may appear simple. Yet many conflicts continue to exist because people have forgotten or not taken sufficient time to examine *all* options open to them. Then the respondents predict the essential probable consequences for each of the alternative actions as well as the chances (odds) for these consequences to occur. This is necessary because a consequence with only a 1 in 1000 chance of occurring does not deserve the same attention as one with a 1 in 2 chance. The respondents next judge the probable consequences as good or not, advantageous or not, worthwhile or not, or preferred or not. They wind up with a mix of consequences with a probability score and a value rating. For example, a remote possibility of a train hitting a school bus (let us estimate this accident at less than a 1 in 2000 chance) may receive undue consideration and cause a holdup in decision making.

To put the conflict into a clear perspective the respondents seek a parallel value conflict. Once again they use the technique of examining an analogy as a way of gaining clarity. Then they seek a general principle based on the conflict at hand and its parallel which, if it exists, will subsume the specific conflict and suggest a way of resolving the conflict.

Whether or not the respondents formulate an acceptable generalization, they must finally take a stand by selecting one of the alternative actions as the one they support for resolving the conflict. The respondents must then justify the positions they have taken. They support their decision or decisions by stating the reasons for choosing one alternative over the others. They state just what in this particular conflict leads them to give priority to equality over liberty, for example, as shown by their choice for a long bus ride for school children over segregated neighborhood schools.

This particular decision does not necessarily mean that if a second value conflict arises between equality and liberty the respondents will choose equality over liberty again. The particulars may be different enough to lead them to shift to a changed ranking of values. Whatever the case, the respondents will know for the next time that they have a precedent where they did indeed decide that equality was a more important value to them than liberty.

Strategy 14: Taking a Stand on an Issue
(Making a Policy or Value Decision)

Questioner	Respondent
1. What precisely is the issue before us?	1. Identifies and describes the issue.
2. What is your stand on the issue at this point?	2. Expresses opinion, position.
3. What are the key words used in talking about this issue?	3. Identifies central concepts.
4. Define the key terms.	4. Defines essential terms for clarity of communication.
5. What are your goals about this situation, your desired state of affairs?	5. Establishes ideal.
6. What are the relevant facts, current and past, on this issue?	6. States pertinent evidence for support of position.
7. How would you implement the stand (action, policy) you take?	7. Examines issue from practical, interactive viewpoint.
8. What are the probable consequences of your stand?	8. Predicts consequences of position taken.

(What is likely to happen
as a result of your action?)

9. What would be your position if you were person X?

10. What are some other
    possible positions to take?

11. What are the probable
    consequences of each of
    these alternatives?

12. In what ways is your stand
    on this issue related to
    another issue or position
    you've taken previously?

13. In light of all these points,
    what stand do you take on
    this issue now?

14. What are your reasons for
    this stand? (What are the
    key points that lead you
    to this position?)

9. Sees issue from another
   perspective.

10. Describes alternatives.

11. Predicts consequences of
    the various alternatives.

12. Sees connection with a
    parallel situation for
    possible general
    principle.

13. Expresses opinion based
    on previous points.

14. Gives reasons, justifies
    the position taken.

Strategy 14 focuses on taking a stand or position on a public policy issue such as nuclear disarmament, legalizing the smoking of marijuana, federal aid to parochial schools, and U.S. support and aid for Israel. Because the taking of a stand in a reasonable way requires consideration of a complex set of variables, this strategy is long in terms of the number of steps and the time needed to complete it. The strategy is also complex in that it requires the respondents to offer definitions, facts, explanations, comparisons, opinions, and justifications.

This strategy initially resembles the previous one. The respondents start, as usual, by identifying and describing just what the issue is. Then, even before defining the key terms connected with this policy issue, the respondents each take an initial stand on the issue. They do so in order to demonstrate the range of positions possible, to acknowledge the fact that people do have opinions on public issues whether or not they arrive at them after careful consideration, and most of all to involve themselves in the issue by requiring a commitment at the outset.

Unless people commit themselves to a stand it is difficult for them to get involved in considering the issue. If they do not take a stand, they do not have a stake in the issue. It would be like playing in a tennis match at Wimbeldon against Billie Jean King and not caring about who wins. You may applaud her when she makes a winning lob down the line or feel good when you serve an ace, but you don't ever get involved in the game or excited and tense as play progresses.

The remaining responses offered by the respondents are keyed into the stands they take. The facts and reasons offered are chosen so as to support the stands taken. If the facts and reasons given are relevant and supportive, then the respondent is being reasonable, for rationality consists of suiting a position with its justification. Thus, the respondents state their goals, then the relevant facts, then their proposed implementation plans, and then the probable consequences of their stands.

Once the respondents have considered their own stands, they proceed to look at the issue from the vantage point of someone else involved in the issue. For example, let us suppose that the issue is U.S. aid for Israel. If all the respondents are Americans, then the questioner may well ask in step 9 "What would be your position if you were Prime Minister of Israel?" and/or "What would be your position if you were President of Egypt?" The respondents must then, through role playing, assume a new opinion or attitude. Next the respondents would offer other alternative stands and their consequences so as to broaden their examination and consideration of the issue.

The final examination occurs as the respondents relate their stands on the issue to their stands on other issues. The question calling for a comparison of stands encourages the respondents to probe even further for consistency in their own beliefs. For example, you may ask in step 12 of the issue on Israel "In what way is your stand on U.S. support to Israel related to your stand on U.S. support of South Korea since the early 1950s?"

Once the respondents have probed the issue in several ways, they are ready to offer their concluding stands on the issue. They have the opportunity and the right to modify their stands in light of the many points raised by everyone. They conclude by offering their reasons for their stands. People with the same stands may offer different reasons. This justification step is necessary in order to assure the rationality of the entire endeavor, for with their responses of justification, the respondents become responsible for their positions.

Strategy 15: Debriefing a Simulation Game
or Other Role Playing Activity

Questioner	*Respondent*
1. Describe some of the specifics that occurred to you during the activity (role playing, simulation), such as decisions you made and how you felt.	1. Describes some details of the activity, making them public knowledge.
2. What did you learn about yourself and others from this activity?	2. States the personal meaning of the activity.
3. What are the key ideas that this activity teaches us?	3. States the concepts or generalizations that give meaning or purpose to the activity.
4. In what ways are the actions, rules, and outcomes of this activity similar to other parts of your life?	4. Compares and contrasts the activity with other events of the world.
5. In what ways can we	5. Suggests modifications

change this activity to make it more like the real events?	which will make the activity a better (closer) simulation.
6. What do you conclude from all of these actions?	6. Summarizes and concludes about the entire activity.

Strategy 15 focuses on discussing the meaning, purposes, or benefits of a role playing activity such as a simulation game, sociodrama, or historic reenactment. In several ways this strategy is similar to previous ones which focus on analyzing a document or value and comparing and contrasting two items. One unique aspect, however, which is detailed below, sets this strategy off from the others and therefore is the reason for acknowledging a separate strategy for debriefing role-playing activities.

The debriefing begins with a question asking the participants to describe some details of the activity. The purpose is threefold: The first is to make public any details that some participants don't know. The second is to allow the participants to ventilate after an active, involving activity. The third is to provide a nonthreatening, concrete basis for talking about what might well have been a tense and emotional experience.

Next comes the analysis of the activity in terms of its meaning. The respondents are asked to state the personal meaning of the activity for them. You ask what the results mean to them and what they learned about themselves as participants in an activity and as people in general. The next question focuses on the cognitive meaning of the activity: You ask about the concepts and generalizations which the activity is designed to teach.

In the third part of the debriefing you analyze the activity in terms of its similarity with other events in life. Without directing the participants attention to this aspect of the activity there would be little, if any, special purpose of conducting a simulation game or sociodrama in the first place. Role playing activities are designed to simulate life, and you are therefore obligated to ask question which lead the respondents to examine the model inherent in the activity. You ask what the individual features of the activity represent and how these elements altogether are similar to other parts of life outside of the particular teaching situation.

Follow the analysis of similarity with a request for modifications. Let us assume that in your examination of the activity the respondents show that a key player often makes a decision contrary to expectations. Your request then would be for a modification of the action and/or rules and/or participants so that the key person can consistently decide as expected. In this way the respondents are suggesting modifications which will bring the activity in closer alignment with that part of life it simulates.

You end your debriefing by asking for an overall conclusion from the respondents. This conclusion or summary is broader than any generalization made in the second part of the strategy. This is because the respondents will now base their conclusion on the analysis of the model presented by the activity itself as well as any suggested modifications of the activity.

Practice Exercise 9
(Refer to Strategies 11, 12, 13, 14, and 15)

1. Suggest a person connected with the field of science whose values your students could analyze.
2. Suggest two classroom happenings related to your students that would yield an opportunity to clarify feelings with your students.
3. Recently a University of Michigan student erroneously voted in an election. (She was thought to live in the township, but she lived just beyond the border. It was not her error.) Backed by a Michigan law the judge considering the contested election requested the young

woman to tell how she voted so he could subtract her vote from the legal ones. She refused to announce her secret vote. What do you see as the value conflict for which your students could suggest a resolution?

4. Suppose that your students are examining the issue of smoking and possessing marijuana. They are to take a stand on this public issue. Suggest four people (see step 9 of strategy 14) from different fields whose positions you could ask your students to consider.

5. Suppose that your students have just completed a simulation of a United Nations committee meeting on the issue of world hunger. Suggest three questions that will direct the students to analyze the similarities between their activity and the United Nations. (See step 4 of Strategy 15.)

SIX

TWENTY-FIVE QUESTIONING DIALOGUES: A MANUAL OF QUESTIONING TECHNIQUES

This chapter presents dialogues for learning and practicing the various questioning techniques that cut across the five general and fifteen specific strategies in the previous chapters. These dialogues are an outgrowth of working with teachers in class and workshop settings to help them improve their ability to question effectively. They are a practical way of involving you in your own improvement.

HOW TO USE THE QUESTIONING DIALOGUES

These questioning dialogues are not simulations. When you use these dialogues in trios, you are not simulating a teaching situation. Rather you are asking questions, responding, and reacting with several other people. What you learn from these exercises you apply to your teaching situation because the training and teaching situations are similar enough to allow and encourage transfer.

On the other hand, you must recognize that these training situations are just that—artificial situations where everyone involved knows that you are asking particular questions in a particular way for a particular purpose. For this reason there is a slight sense of unreality to the training situations that makes questioning your colleagues a bit strained. Nevertheless, without exercises it would be virtually impossible for a group of people to learn and practice techniques without using their students as guinea pigs.

The first item of training is for you to find two or three other people who are interested in self-improvement. This will give you a trio or quartet which I have found to be the best arrangement for these exercises. Pairs do not yield enough input, nor do they allow any single person the opportunity to observe what others are doing and thus to benefit by reflecting on their actions and by offering them helpful feedback. Quintets do not offer enough opportunities for each person to practice asking questions. Trios and quartets are ideal because each participant has many opportunities to ask questions and also during the same exercises to gain insight through observing, giving, and receiving feedback.

The second item of training is to accept the following guidelines which set the ground rules and tone of the interaction with your colleagues. They establish a serious, working tone of active involvement that is nonthreatening. This allows and encourages each person the opportunity to participate, err, revise, try again, and talk freely with the other trainees.

Guidelines for Using a Questioning Dialogue

1. Conduct the dialogue—don't just talk about it. Do it, get the feeling, see what happens, and then talk about it.
2. Read through the entire questioning dialogue and its commentary so that you understand what it is you're to do. Then do the exercise. Consult the steps and distinctive pattern as you proceed if you have any problems.
3. Give positive, helpful feedback to your training colleagues. Con-

centrate on what they did *right*. Reinforce the positive, don't focus on the negative.

4. After you conduct a dialogue or set of dialogues, debrief what you did. Discuss with your training colleagues ways to apply the idea(s) to your own teaching situation. For example, ask where you can utilize this idea, how, and when. When someone else asks you for a suggestion, be specific in your response as a way of triggering further suggestions.

5. During your feedback and discussion period, raise problems that you have noticed so that all of you can offer clarifications and solutions. Your colleagues and you will benefit as you pool your resources. Don't be bashful.

6. Note suggestions as you go along for possible future questioning dialogues that will be helpful to you. Later on you can design new exercises and try them out.

The third item of training is to assign each trainee an ID letter. One person is A, the next B, and the third C. (I refer to a training group as a trio for simplicity's sake. If you have a quartet, then you will have a person D also.) The fourth and final item of training is to understand the general format of conducting these dialogues. Let us take Questioning Dialogue 1 as an example for explanation.

Questioning Dialogue 1 as an Illustration:

1. Trio decides on a common topic for questions.
2. Each person writes at least two questions.
3. Trio follows this cyclical pattern:
   A: Questions.
   B: Responds.
   C: Responds and/or reacts if desires.
   A: Waits to a count of five and nods to indicate closure.
4. Trio rotates and repeats cycle.
5. Trio debriefs.

In step 1 the trio quickly decides on a common topic in which they are interested so they can talk with ease to each other. In step 2 each person writes two questions as a way of getting prepared and involved in the topic. Step 3 offers the central pattern of the dialogue. This pattern means that person A asks a question of person B. Person B responds and person C may also respond if C wants to. As always, B and C may then react to each other if they wish. (Reacting is different from responding. When you respond, you try to answer the question asked or you indicate that you don't know the answer. When you react to a question or a response, you comment on it. You can praise, agree, disagree, expand, elaborate, criticize, or reject it. You can make several types of comments in one reaction if you wish.) You can react to a question ("That's a good question"), or to a response ("You're right and I want to add that I like modern dance just as much as ballet"), but you can only respond to a question.

After B and C have responded and reacted, A waits silently (counting to five) and then nods to B and C to indicate closure. Then, as indicated in step 4, the trio rotates in this pattern, first with B as questioner and C as respondent and then with C as questioner and A as respondent. When the cycle is completed in this way, each trainee will ask one question, respond to one question directly, and possibly respond to a question asked initially to another person. Also, since each person has prepared at least two questions to ask according to step 2, the trio will begin a second cycle and repeat the above pattern. In step 5 the trio debriefs, talking about what happened during the two cycles. This debriefing is essential, as indicated in the fourth and fifth guidelines for using a questioning dialogue.

The other dialogues follow the general format of this first one. With an understanding of this one, you will be able to follow the steps of each of the twenty-five questioning dialogues which follow. Each dialogue has a specific purpose as indicated in its title.

Questioning Dialogue 1:
Wait-Time After Other Speaker

1. Trio decides on a common topic for questions not in yes/no format.
2. Each person writes at least two questions not in yes/no format.
3. Trio follows this cycle pattern:
    A: Questions.
    B: Responds.
    C: Responds and/or reacts if desires.
    A: Waits to a count of five and nods to indicate closure.
4. Trio rotates and repeats cycle.
5. Trio debriefs.

Questioning dialogue 1 teaches you to utilize the concept of wait-time in your questioning. Research on teaching indicates how an apparently slight change in teacher action can have significant effects on what happens in the classroom during teaching. Rowe[1] and Lake[2] investigated the amount of time teachers wait when asking a question. They found that if students do not begin a response within one second, teachers usually repeat the question or call upon other students to respond. Also, after students respond, teachers usually wait slightly less than one second before reacting to the response, asking another question, or launching a new topic. According to studies by Rowe and by Lake, when teachers increased their wait-time to three to five seconds, the following significant results occurred:

For students; the length of student responses increased; the number of unsolicited but appropriate responses increased; failure to respond decreased; confidence as reflected

---

[1]Mary Budd Rowe, "Science, Silence, and Sanctions," *Science and Children*, 6 (September 1969): 11-13; idem, "Wait-Time and Rewards as Instructional Variables: Their Influence on Language, Logic, and Fate Control," abstract of a paper presented to the National Association for Research in Science Teaching, April 1972; idem. *Teaching Science as Continuous Inquiry* (New York: McGraw-Hill Book Company, 1973), pp. 243-73.
[2]John H. Lake, "The Influence of Wait-Time on the Verbal Dimension of Student Inquiry Behavior" (Doctoral dissertation, Rutgers University, 1973).

in fewer inflected responses increased, and fewer responses had the tone of "Is that what you want?"; the incidence of speculative thinking increased; the incidence of offering alternative explanations increased; more evidence followed by or preceded by inference statements occurred; the number of questions asked by students increased and the number of (science) experiments they proposed increased; teacher-centered show and tell decreased, and student-student comparing increased; the number of responses from "slow" students increased so that there was a greater variety of students participating; the incidence of students responding with congruent and more complex answers occurred (ascending modal congruence increased); the incidence of conversation sequences increased (sequences involving three or more related utterances increased in number).

For teachers; teachers became more flexible in their discourse, asked fewer questions, increased the variety of their questions, and improved their expectations of performance of "slow" students.

These results show that just a slight change in the pacing of the discussion, done by increasing the teacher's wait-time, led to changes in pedagogical roles and cognitive performance. Students started asking more questions and participating more, as well as offering alternative explanations, increasing speculative thinking, and offering more complete responses. The knowledge of such research and then the implementation of a wait-time schedule of three to five seconds will certainly aid you in using any of the general or specific strategies offered earlier and in using the techniques still to be offered.

The key points about wait-time involve the results of allowing the students time to talk. It is true that, in general, students will talk if the teacher allows them to talk. The effect of teacher talk is to cut off student talk. Students usually do not interrupt teachers. When a teacher talks, whether reacting, responding, questioning, or presenting information, that teacher in effect prohibits the students from talking. When the teacher has the floor, the students are silent. And following the "classroom law of inertia," a student who is silent tends to remain silent. Thus, if the teacher does not begin to talk after each student finishes, the teacher nonverbally encourages the students to talk. As mentioned earlier in Chapter 5, there exists a significant need for and benefit from having students talk as part of the classroom teaching situation.

Questioning Dialogue 2:
Wait Time After Own Question

1. Trio decides on a common topic for questions.
2. Each person writes at least two questions.
3. Trio follows this cycle pattern:
    - **A:** Questions and waits to a count of five.
    - **B:** Waits to a count of five; C waits also.
    - **B:** Responds.
    - **C:** Responds and/or reacts if desires.
    - **A:** Waits to a count of five and nods to indicate closure.
4. Trio rotates and repeats cycle.
5. Trio debriefs.

Questioning Dialogue 2 enlists the respondent's help in teaching the questioner to wait after asking a question. (See the commentary on wait-time in questioning dialogue 1.) The questioner waits to a count of five and succeeds in getting B to respond without repeating the question or urging B in any way. This exercise complements the preceding one by teaching the questioner to wait after asking a question as well as waiting after the respondent talks.

Questioning Dialogue 3:
Wait Time and Restating Question

1. Trio decides on a common topic for questions.

2. Each person writes at least two questions.
3. Trio follows this cycle pattern:
     A: Questions and waits to a count of five.
     B: Does not respond; C does not respond.
     A: Restates the question at the count of five.
     B: Responds.
     C: Responds and/or reacts, if desires.
     A: Waits to a count of five and nods to indicate closure.
4. Trio rotates and repeats cycle.
5. Trio debriefs.

Questioning Dialogue 3 teaches the questioner to wait and not to lose track of the question or strategy being used at the time. Teachers often become flustered when a student does not respond immediately. They then, as pointed out in the commentary for Questioning Dialogue 1, call on another student or ask another question. Either way, the teachers may break their planned strategy. By learning to restate the same question, either to the same student or to another student, the questioner sticks with the planned strategy. The questioner does not create a gap in the strategic responses by asking another question due to being caught off guard by an un-answered question. If the questioner asks another question prematurely, the new response may not be forthcoming, may be only partial, or may not be understood by other students because a missing link was created in the strategy. The questioner may thus inadvertently cause confusion in the minds of the respondents because a response needed for the flow of the strategy is not available to the students to help them in making connections.

If the questioner feels that the respondent didn't under-stand the question and hence did not respond, the questioner can rephrase the question rather than restate it. The trouble here is that the rephrased question is often a different ques-tion. In rephrasing, the questioner must be careful not to change the meaning of the question. For this reason it is easier and safer to simply restate the question. The objective is to maintain a position in the planned strategy rather than let a detailed plan go down the drain during the intensity of the teaching situation.

Questioning Dialogue 4:
Strong and Pertinent Positive Reaction

1. Trio decides on a common topic for questions.
2. Each person writes at least two questions.
3. Trio follows this cycle pattern:
    - **A:** Questions.
    - **B:** Waits to a count of five; C/waits also.
    - **B:** Responds.
    - **C:** Responds and/or reacts, if desires.
    - **A:** Waits to a count of five and reacts with a strong and pertinent positive rating of B and C.
4. Trio rotates and repeats cycle.
5. Trio debriefs.

Questioning Dialogue 4 teaches the questioner to react to the respondent in a strong, positive way. The common way for teachers to react is with a mildly positive word or phrase such as "Alright," "O.K.," or "Hm-Hm." This is different from a strong positive reaction such as "Absolutely," "Excellent answer," or "An appropriate remark." Respondents naturally react differently to a strong positive rating than a mildly positive rating. Respondents feel better when the rating is stronger and not the usual, common, mild one which teachers often say quickly, somewhat softly, and routinely as if by habit and without much conviction.

The questioner in this dialogue can react either with strong words such as "Absolutely" and "Precisely," or phrases reflecting the particular contribution such as "An appropriate remark," "You hit the nail on the head with that response," "Your comment was timely and to the point," or "Your phrasing was correct and on target." Of course the questioner can use both styles. In either case, the questioner conveys the message that the remarks are positive, strong, and pertinent, giving evidence that the questioner listened to the respondent and framed an appropriate rating.

Questioning Dialogue 5:
Eliciting Multiple
Responses

1. Trio decides on a common topic for questions.
2. Each person writes at least two starting questions, each of a type that can elicit several (three to four) possible responses.
3. Trio follows this cycle pattern:
    A: Questions using the first starting question.
    B: Waits to a count of five; C waits also.
    B: Responds.
    C: Reacts, if desires.
    A: Questions again with "Another one, please," or "Give me more like that, please," or a similar variation.
    C: Responds.
    B: Reacts if desires.
    A: Questions again with "Another one, please."
    B: Responds.
    C: Reacts, if desires.
    A: Waits to a count of five and either nods to indicate closure or reacts with a strong and pertinent rating.
4. Trio rotates and repeats cycle (using second starting question.)
5. Trio debriefs.

Questioning Dialogue 5 teaches the questioner to elicit multiple responses from the respondents as a means of increasing participation and peer teaching. The questioner may ask a question like "Name a past President of the U.S." Such a question has many possible correct responses, and the questioner can elicit multiple responses before asking a different question or reacting to the respondent. Other examples are:

a.   Define a word which begins with the letter 's'.
b.   Explain a natural event such as rain, fog, snow, volcano, or hurricane.
c.   Select any professional or amateur athlete and rate that athlete as a candidate for Sportsperson of the Year.
d.   State an item used daily which we import from Europe, Africa, Asia, or South America.

Ryan, in his research on questioning, showed that when teachers asked such questions and elicited multiple student responses, the students achieved in a superior manner. Ryan explains the superior achievement in his research classes by claiming that students learn from the responses of their classmates. Furthermore, "certainly within a classroom that numbers about thirty or so students (i.e., the size of the treatment groups in the present study), not every student will be called upon on each question; but still, if enough students are called upon, it may become clear to all students that they are capable, and indeed are expected to participate in the instructional activities."[3]

With this exercise the questioner learns to elicit at least three responses (the questioner or trio may decide to elicit at least four responses) with a certain type of question. This eliciting of multiple responses is an excellent technique to employ in a plateaus strategy or an inductive strategy (see Chapter 4) when building up a foundation of data for all respondents to use.

Questioning Dialogue 6: Plateaus Questioning

1.   Trio decides on a common topic for questions.
2.   Each person writes at least two starting questions.

[3]Frank L. Ryan, "The Effects on Social Studies Achievement of Multiple Student Responding to Different Levels of Questioning," *The Journal of Experimental Education*, 42, no. 4 (Summer 1974), 71-75.

3. Trio follows this cycle pattern:

    A: Questions (using the first starting question).

    B: Waits to a count of five; C waits also.

    B: Responds.

    C: Reacts, if desires.

    A: Questions again on the same plateau as first question. (See below for examples and clarification.)

    C: Responds.

    B: Reacts, if desires.

    A: Questions again on the same plateau as first and second question. (See below for examples and clarification.)

    B: Responds.

    C: Reacts, if desires.

    A: Waits to a count of five and either nods to indicate closure or reacts with a strong and positive rating.

4. Trio rotates and repeats cycle (using second starting question).

5. Trio debriefs.

Questioning Dialogue 6 teaches the questioner to use the plateaus strategy (see Chapter 4). While this dialogue is similar to the preceding one, the difference lies in the second and third questions asked. In the preceding exercise the questioner asks the same question three times by using the expression "Another one, please." In this exercise the questioner actually asks three different questions. The second and third questions are deliberately of the same cognitive type as the first question, however, and if you plotted the progression of questions you would have a figure resembling the plateaus diagram shown in Figure 2 of Chapter 4.

For example, suppose your first question is "Name a past President of the U.S." Your second question might be "To what political party did this President belong?" Your third question might be "Give one well-known event that occurred during his term of office." In this way all three questions are different but are of the same cognitive type. They form the beginning part of a plateaus strategy. The questioner can here make use of the plateaus strategy described earlier. This is essential to

working in an inductive manner where students can base conclusions on data already elicited.

Questioning Dialogue 7: Peaks Questioning

1. Trio decides on a common topic for questions.
2. Each person writes at least two starting questions.
3. Trio follows this cycle pattern:
    A: Questions (using the first starting question).
    B: Waits to a count of five; C waits also.
    B: Responds.
    C: Reacts, if desires.
    A: Questions again, seeking a comparison (so as to begin a peaks strategy by building on the first question).
    B: Responds.
    C: Reacts, if desirds.
    A: Questions again, seeking a cause or conclusion (so as to form a three-step peaks strategy by building on the two previous questions).
    B: Responds.
    C: Reacts, if desires.
    A: Waits to a count of five and either nods to indicate closure or reacts with a strong and positive rating.
4. Trio rotates and repeats cycle (using second starting question).
5. Trio debriefs.

Questioning Dialogue 7 teaches the questioner to use the peaks strategy (see Chapter 4). Whereas in the preceding exercise the second and third questions are of the same type, in this exercise the questioner asks a different question each time to elicit a different cognitive process. If you were to plot these questions, you would have a figure resembling the peaks diagram shown earlier in Figure 4–1 of Chapter 4.

For example, suppose your first question is "Name a past

President of the U.S." Your second question might be "In what way is he similar to our current President?" This question asks the respondent to make a comparison, thereby forming the beginning of a peaks strategy. Your third question in a three-step peaks strategy might be "What are the reasons for these two Presidents being alike?" Here you ask the respondent to offer an explanation of causes. If you as questioner wish, it is possible to develop a four-step peaks strategy. In either case it is necessary to develop a recognizable and coherent peaks strategy. This is essential when probing with a respondent on a given topic.

Questioning Dialogue 8:
Plateaus and Peaks Questioning

1. Trio decides on a common topic for questions.
2. Each person writes at least one starting question.
3. Trio follows this cycle pattern:
   - **A:** Questions.
   - **B:** Waits to a count of five; C waits also.
   - **B:** Responds.
   - **C:** Reacts, if desires.
   - **A:** Questions again on the same plateau.
   - **C:** Responds.
   - **B:** Reacts, if desires.
   - **A:** Questions again on the same plateau.
   - **B:** Responds.
   - **C:** Reacts, if desires.
   - **A:** Questions with a question of a different type to move off the plateau onto the beginning of another one.
   - **C:** Responds.
   - **B:** Reacts, if desires.
   - **A:** Waits to a count of five and either nods to indicate closure or reacts with a strong and positive rating.

4. Trio rotates and repeats cycle, if possible, built on another starting question.
5. Trio debriefs.

Questioning Dialogue 8 combines the features of the three preceding dialogues. This is a four-step pattern in which the questioner begins by developing a plateaus strategy and only shifts to the next plateau with a probing question of another cognitive type. The questioner learns to develop a plateau and to move from it to another plateau only after staying on the first plateau for at least three questions.

For example, suppose that your first question is "Name a past President of the U.S." Your second question might be "To what political party did this President belong?" Your third question might be "Give one well-known event which occurred during his term of office." Your fourth question, which moves you onto another plateau, might be "Compare this President with the current President in terms of this major event." In this way you stay on one plateau for three questions and then begin a second plateau with a question calling for the respondent to compare two Presidents. These four questions serve to teach you to ask a probing question only after some data have already been elicited from the respondents.

Questioning Dialogue 9:
Involving Multiple Respondents

1. Trio decides on a common topic for questions.
2. Each person writes at least two starting questions asking for an explanation of how to do something.
3. Trio follows this cycle pattern:
    A: Questions.
    B: Waits to a count of five; C waits also.

B: Responds partially, deliberately leaving out a small step in the procedure.

A: Questions C, "Will you please add to that?" or the equivalent.

C: Responds.

A: Questions B, "If you have anything else you wish to add, please do so."

B: Responds.

A: Waits to a count of five and either nods to indicate closure or reacts with a strong and positive rating.

4. Trio rotates and repeats cycle (with second starting question).
5. Trio debriefs.

Questioning Dialogue 9 supplements the preceding ones which teach the questioner to utilize the plateaus strategy. This exercise teaches the questioner to involve more participants in responding to a given question. To do this, we enlist the help of the first respondent (person B) by requesting that only a partial explanation of the procedure be given. In this way the second respondent (person C) will surely have something to add when asked since all have agreed upon a commonly known procedure. For example, the trio may agree on explaining how to fix a flat tire, how to cook spaghetti, how to park a car, or how to address an envelope.

The benefit of this technique derives from having respondents help each other out (peer teaching), and offers the questioner the opportunity to diagnose the respondents' knowledge of the procedure. The questioner does not correct or expand on B's explanation immediately. The questioner involves other respondents and diagnoses the situation at the same time. If there is a need for the questioner to help out in completing the explanation to the satisfaction of the respondents it is always possible for the questioner to do so after several respondents have attempted explanations. See Strategies 7 and 10 in Chapter 5 for comments on eliciting missing details in an explanation. See also the commentary related to Questioning Dialogue 5 which focuses on multiple responses to a given question.

Questioning Dialogue 10: Clarifying Probe

1. Trio decides on a common moral or public policy issue for questions.
2. Each person writes at least one starting question calling for an *opinion* not in yes/no format.
3. Trio follows this cycle pattern:
   - **A:** Questions.
   - **B:** Waits to a count of five; C waits also.
   - **B:** Responds with an opinion.
   - **C:** Reacts, if desires.
   - **A:** Questions B or C with a probe: "What do you mean by_____?" or "Please clarify your use of the expression_____." or some other equivalent question.
   - **B or C:** Responds, depending upon who was asked.
   - **B or C:** Reacts, if desires.
   - **A:** Waits to a count of five and either nods to indicate closure or reacts with a strong and positive rating.
4. Trio rotates and repeats cycle, if possible, built on another starting question.
5. Trio debriefs.

Questioning Dialogue 10 begins a set of exercises which focuses on teaching the questioner several probing techniques. The questioner often wishes to probe the respondent's remarks, especially in an explaining or valuing strategy. The most common probe is "Why?" The why question has two distinct disadvantages, however, which lead to the need for a wider repertoire of probing questions. First, the why question is so overworked that it borders on the routine, thus losing its impact as a probe. Because of the commonness of the why probe, there is no questioning dialogue devoted to it here.

Second (and more important), the why question, when used with a moral or public policy issue, is a threatening question. It calls for the respondent to justify a personal opinion. Such a question challenges the personal beliefs of the respondent by requesting reasons for the opinion offered. This is much more threatening than the request for reasons concerning causal explanation of a natural event. It is much more threatening to a respondent for a questioner to ask "Why do you support the legalization of marijuana?" than it is to ask "Why did it rain yesterday?" It is all the more threatening for a questioner to ask a why question in regard to an interpersonal issue. (For example, "Why do you dislike me?") With such a why question, the respondent is in a defensive position, and this does not encourage or foster open communication.

For these reasons the questioner needs to be able to probe in a minimally threatening or nonthreatening manner. Though all probes may threaten the respondent somewhat, some probes significantly reduce or remove the threat. Because of this, Questioning Dialogue 10 teaches the clarifying probe. This exercise teaches the questioner to ask the respondent or reactor to clarify a remark already made. It is the first dialogue focusing on a set of probes to aid the questioner.

Suppose that your first question was "What is your personal opinion regarding governmental sterilization of criminals?" Suppose further than the respondent says "I think the government should sterilize serious sex offenders." Your probing question may be "Would you clarify what you mean by 'serious sex offenders'?" You may phrase the question differently if you wish as long as you request the respondent to clarify something said.

In this way the questioner can probe in a less threatening or nonthreatening way. The questioner thus takes into consideration not only the cognitive type of question but also the affective result of asking a question. The clarifying probe offers the questioner one technique for probing a comment by a respondent or reactor.

Questioning Dialogue 11: How-Arrived Probe

1. Trio decides on a common moral or public policy issue for questions.

2. Each person write at least one starting question calling for an *opinion* not in yes/no format.
3. Trio follows this cycle pattern:
    A: Questions.
    B: Waits to a count of five; C waits also.
    B: Responds with an opinion.
    C: Reacts, if desires.
    A: Questions B or C with a "how-arrived" probe: "How did you arrive at your opinion?" or some equivalent question.
    B or C: Responds, depending upon who was asked.
    B or C: Reacts, if desires.
    A: Waits to a count of five and either nods to indicate closure or reacts with a strong and positive rating.
4. Trio rotates and repeats cycle, if possible, built on another starting question.
5. Trio debriefs.

Questioning Dialogue 11 teaches another probing technique that is not commonly used. Nevertheless, this probe is a powerful one in that it requires the respondent to consider the *process* (as opposed to the *reasons*) utilized in forming an opinion. This probe is therefore called the "how-arrived" probe.

Suppose your first question was "What is your personal opinion regarding governmental sterilization of criminals?" Suppose further that the respondent says "I think the government should sterilize serious sex offenders." Your "how-arrived" probe may be "Tell us how you arrived at your opinion of sterilizing sex offenders." You may phrase this probe differently as long as you request the respondent to relate the *process* used in arriving at that opinion.

A note of caution: Many persons are so unfamiliar with this probe that they don't know how to respond to it properly. People often respond to a how-arrived probe as if it is a why probe seeking causes. A person may therefore respond "I think they ought to be sterilized because then they won't perpetuate themselves." Such a response is not appropriate because it doesn't deal with the *process* used by the respondent. It is an answer to a question which you haven't asked. A congruent response (not correct, but congruent, since with such a question the issue of correctness is irrelevant) might be "Well, I asked several people I know and respect; I discussed the issue with them—one was a judge—and I accept their point of view as mine."

If you do receive an incongruent response to your how-arrived probe you will need to gently reject the response as incongruent, explain what you want, and ask the question again. As your students become accustomed to this type of probe you will not need to explain that you want a process response rather than a causal response.

A congruent response to a how-arrived probe offers you as questioner and other people as reactors the opportunity to talk about how the respondent arrived at the opinion or conclusion offered. As you all examine the process used by the respondent, you will aid the respondent in thinking through the issue again. Such a way of eliciting rethinking is less threatening to the respondent than requesting the reasons for holding the opinion offered.

Questioning Dialogue 12: Inter-Issue Probe

1. Trio decides on a common moral or public policy issue for questions.
2. Each person writes at least one starting question calling for an opinion not in yes/no format.
3. Trio follows this cycle pattern:
   - **A:** Questions.
   - **B:** Waits to a count of five; C waits also.
   - **B:** Responds with an opinion.
   - **C:** Reacts, if desires.
   - **A:** Questions B or C with an inter-issue probe "How is your opinion on this issue related to your opinion on the issue of_____?" or some equivalent question.

B or C: Responds.
B or C: Reacts, if desires.
    A: Waits to a count of five and either nods to indicate closure or reacts with a strong and positive rating.
4. Trio rotates and repeats cycle, if possible, built on another starting question.
5. Trio debriefs.

Questioning Dialogue 12 teaches a third not commonly used probing technique. The questioner asks the respondent to think about the opinion in light of an opinion held on a related moral or public policy issue. This probe is therefore called the inter-issue probe.

Suppose that the response to your first question was "I think the government should sterilize serious sex offenders." Rather than ask "Why?", "What do you mean by 'serious sex offenders'?", or "How did you arrive at that opinion?" as you would with the previously mentioned probes, the inter-issue probe would prompt you to ask "How is your opinion on the sterilization of sex offenders related to your view on capital punishment of convicted murderers?" Of course, you may phrase this probe differently or relate the response to another issue pertinent to the respondent, such as the rehabilitation of criminals and the sterilizing of feeble-minded people.

After the respondent has related the response on the sterilizing of sex offenders to another opinion, you as questioner and other people as reactors can explore the similarities and differences in the positions taken. The relating of one issue to another and the subsequent exploring of the relationship offers an excellent method for everyone, especially the respondent, to think through the issue again.

Questioning Dialogue 13: Role-Switch Probe

1. Trio decides on a common moral or public policy issue for questions.

2. Each person writes at least one starting question calling for an opinion not in yes/no format.
3. Trio follows this cycle pattern:
    A: Questions.
    B: Waits to a count of five; C waits also.
    B: Responds with an opinion.
    C: Reacts, if desires.
    A: Questions B or C with a role-switch probe "If you were_____, what would be your opinion on this issue?"
    B or C: Responds.
    B or C: Reacts, if desires.
    A: Waits to a count of five and either nods to indicate closure or reacts with a strong and positive rating.
4. Trio rotates and repeats cycle, if possible, built on another starting question.
5. Trio debriefs.

Questioning Dialogue 13 teaches a fourth probing technique. The questioner asks the respondent to view the issue from another vantage point. The respondent assumes the role of another person, views the issue, and gives an opinion which may be different from the personal one given previously. This probe is therefore called the role-switch probe.

Suppose the response to your first question was "I think the government should sterilize serious sex offenders." In using this role-switch probe you might ask "If you were the criminal's spouse, what would be your opinion on sterilization?" Or you might, as a substitute for the role of spouse, ask about other roles: the criminal's mother, the criminal's father, the criminal himself/herself, the president of the American Civil Liberties Union, or the sex offender's victim. You may phrase the question differently, of course, as long as you request the respondent to respond from another identifiable perspective.

The benefit of the role-switch probe derives from having the respondent view the issue from that other perspective. To permit and facilitate this pluralistic view, the questioner utilizes the well-known technique of role playing. The questioner need not set up a complicated scenario, however.

Rather, the questioner simply requests the respondent to pretend to be someone else. The questioner can request the respondent to take a series of roles so as to elicit a variety of responses to a given question.

After the respondent offers an additional opinion or opinions via this role-switch probe, you as questioner and other people as reactors can explore these opinions. It is especially provoking for the respondent to think through the issue again if the various roles taken elicit different opinions. Everyone can then explore the factors that lead to the various opinions taken by different people.

Questioning Dialogue 14: Specifics Probe

1. Trio decides on a common moral or public policy issue for questions.
2. Each person writes at least one starting question calling for an opinion.
3. Trio follows this cycle pattern:
   - **A:** Questions.
   - **B:** Waits to a count of five; C waits also.
   - **B:** Responds with an opinion.
   - **C:** Reacts, if desires.
   - **A:** Questions B or C with a specific probe "What is it specifically about_____that you favor/disfavor?" or "What is it specifically that_____does that you favor/disfavor?"
   - **B or C:** Responds.
   - **B or C:** Reacts, if desires.
   - **A:** Waits to a count of five and either nods to indicate closure or reacts with a strong and positive rating.
4. Trio rotates and repeats cycle, if possible, built on another starting question.
5. Trio debriefs.

Questioning Dialogue 14 teaches a fifth probing technique. It is a subtle one, not commonly used, which often switches the discourse from the evaluative mode to the empirical mode. (See Chapter 2.) The questioner asks the respondent to specify which details in the broad issue are approved or disapproved of, agreed or disagreed with, favored or disfavored. This probe is therefore called the specifics probe.

Suppose that your first question was "Do you approve of the President's Middle East policy?" Suppose further that the respondent says "No." With the specifics probe you might then ask "What are the specifics of the policy that you disapprove of?" The respondent must then specify the details of the Middle East policy and in so doing will have the opportunity to think through the issue in a focused way.

If your topic deals with justice, you might ask as your starting question "Do you believe that the United Nations is a just organization?" Suppose that the respondent says "No." You might follow with a specifics probe, asking "What specifically does the United Nations do that is not just?" The respondent must then focus on specific actions taken by the United Nations. Such a probing of specifics requests that the respondent shift to talking about observable behavior. This type of discourse is not as threatening to the respondent since it requires a description of behavior rather than justification of opinion by giving reasons.

After the respondent lists the specifics, you as questioner and other people as reactors have the opportunity to explore whichever details the respondent mentions as well as the descriptions offered of the details. The discourse which follows focuses not on the opinion of the respondent, but on observable characteristics or observable behavior. This subtle shift from the evaluative mode to the empirical mode facilitates talk among people, especially people threatened by having to justify their opinions in public.

Questioning Dialogue 15: Elaboration Probe

1.   Trio decides on a common moral or public policy issue for questions.

2. Each person writes at least one starting question calling for an opinion.
3. Trio follows this cycle pattern:
   - **A:** Questions.
   - **B:** Waits to a count of five; C waits also.
   - **B:** Responds with an opinion and some type of justification (explicit or implicit) which gives support to the opinion.
   - **C:** Reacts, if desires.
   - **A:** Questions B or C with an elaboration probe "Please elaborate on your remarks," or "Say more about that, please," or the equivalent.
   - **B or C:** Responds.
   - **B or C:** Reacts, if desires.
   - **A:** Waits to a count of five and either nods to indicate closure or reacts with a strong and positive rating.
4. Trio rotates and repeats cycle, if possible, built on another starting question.
5. Trio debriefs.

Questioning Dialogue 15 teaches the questioner to use a nondirective probe. The questioner does not probe for specifics, reasons, or relations. Rather the questioner takes an obvious neutral position by simply requesting the respondent to elaborate on remarks already made. Hence the name elaboration probe.

Suppose that your first question was "Do you approve of the President's Middle East policy?" Suppose further that the respondent says "No, I don't like his cooperation with the Russians." You might follow with a nondirective elaboration probe by asking "Would you please say more about that?" or "Please elaborate." The respondent is then free to talk in any chosen direction—about the Russians, about cooperating with the Russians, or about other disapproved of aspects of the Middle East policy. The respondent can cite specifics or talk in broad terms. You have been neutral and nondirective, and the respondent may proceed as desired.

The benefit of the elaboration probe comes from allowing the respondent free rein in replying to the question. The questioner simply energizes the respondent, but the respondent chooses the direction. This situation offers the questioner the opportunity to find out what's important to the respondent by diagnosing not only the content of the original response but also the direction and type of the second response. Does the respondent elaborate by giving reasons, specifics, processes, or relationships with other policy issues? Does the respondent elaborate at all?

The elaboration probe is considered mild because it is nondirective. It conveys little threat in that it does not request justification or a specific type of response as the other probes do. You can utilize it best after the respondent has offered only brief or partial remarks. You can employ this probe also as a vehicle for encouraging a shy respondent to participate more in the discussion of a given topic.

Questioning Dialogue 16:
Implementation Probe

1. Trio decides on a common public policy issue for questions.
2. Each person writes at least one starting question calling for a policy decision.
3. Trio follows this cycle pattern:
    A: Questions.
    B: Waits to a count of five; C waits also.
    B: Responds with a decision expressing a stand on the public policy issue at hand.
    C: Questions B or C with an implementation probe "Please tell us how you will (would) implement this decision."
    B or C: Responds.
    B or C: Reacts, if desires.
    A: Waits to a count of five and either nods to indicate closure or reacts with a strong and positive rating.
4. Trio rotates and repeats cycle, if possible, built on another starting question.

5. Trio debriefs.

Questioning Dialogue 16 teaches the questioner to focus on what lies ahead of rather than on what lies behind a response. The questioner accepts the response for what it is and concentrates on how to implement the decision now that it is made. This probe therefore is called the implementation probe.

Suppose that your first question is "What is your stand on nuclear disarmament?" (See Strategy 14 in Chapter 5 for leading respondents to such a question.) Suppose further that the respondent says "I believe that we need worldwide nuclear disarmament or else there may be no world." You might follow with an implementation probe such as "What steps would you take to bring about worldwide disarmament?" Such a probe requires the respondent to consider the issue further by thinking about implementing the decision rather than defending it.

The hidden message in the implementation probe is the implicit acceptance of the response. The questioner does not challenge the decision made by asking for reasons, specifics, or processes that led to the decision. The questioner accepts the decision for what it is and moves forward with it by asking what the respondent will or would do next. This hidden message is one key benefit of the probe. It is a hidden, but nevertheless important, benefit.

A second benefit of this probe stems from pushing the issue forward. Whereas other probes look backward (why and how-arrived probes), and others keep the discourse at the status quo (role-switch and possibly clarifying probes), the implementation probe requires the respondent to leave the evaluative mode and move to the empirical procedure mode. The discourse focuses on the future action needed to make the decision a reality. Such discourse has a vibrant quality to it because it necessitates planning and the use of if/then type thinking. Such discourse promotes involvement and participation by respondent and reactors.

Questioning Dialogue 17: Consequences Probe

1. Trio decides on a common moral or public policy issue for questions.
2. Each person writes at least one starting question calling for a moral or policy decision.
3. Trio follows this cycle pattern:
   - **A:** Questions.
   - **B:** Waits to a count of five; C waits also.
   - **B:** Responds with a statement expressing a decision on the moral or public policy issue chosen.
   - **C:** Reacts, if desires.
   - **A:** Questions B or C with a consequences probe "What are the probable consequences of taking that stand?" or "What will be the effects of that decision?"
   - **B or C:** Responds.
   - **B or C:** Reacts.
   - **A:** Waits to a count of five and either nods to indicate closure or reacts with a strong and positive rating.
4. Trio rotates and repeats cycle, if possible, built on another starting question.
5. Trio debriefs.

Questioning Dialogue 17 teaches the questioner to focus on what lies ahead of rather than on what lies behind a response. The questioner accepts the response for what it is and then requests the respondent to comment on the probable consequences of the decision made. This probe is therefore called the consequences probe.

The emphasis is on *probable* consequences or effects because in most cases it is impossible to know exactly what will be the consequences of a given decision, act, or event. To explore probable consequences is both refreshing and illuminating. When dealing with moral or public policy issues, the consequences may be personal or social. They include what will happen to the decision maker and what will happen to other people concerned with or touched by the decision.

Suppose that the respondent says in response to your first question "I believe that we need worldwide nuclear disarmament or else there may be no world." Rather than follow with an implementation or any other probe, you might ask a consequences probe: "If there is worldwide disarmament, what will be the probable effects on world economy and military planning?" The respondent must then focus on the future in terms of what will result in the economic and military spheres once the threat of nuclear warfare is gone.

The benefit of the consequences probe arises from the hidden message of accepting the respondent's remarks for what they are while getting the respondent to see the effects of a decision. One of the marks of rational decision making is the consideration of probable consequences before making the decision. If the consequences of a particular decision are not desirable, then there is good reason not to make that decision. If the consequences are desirable, then there is good reason to make that decision. By using a consequences probe, the questioner helps the respondent to learn rational decision making.

Questioning Dialogue 18: Parallel Case Probe

1. Trio decides on a common moral or public policy issue for questions.
2. Each person writes at least one starting question calling for an opinion.
3. Trio follows this cycle pattern:
    - **A:** Questions.
    - **B:** Waits to a count of five; C waits also.
    - **B:** Responds with an opinion and some type of justification (explicit or implicit) which gives support to the opinion.
    - **C:** Reacts, if desires.
    - **A:** Questions B or C with a parallel case probe "Would you give another situation where you've taken a similar position," or an equivalent question.
    - **B or C:** Responds.
    - **B or C:** Reacts, if desires.

A: Waits to a count of five and either nods to indicate closure or reacts with a strong and positive rating.

4. Trio rotates and repeats cycle, if possible, built on another starting question.
5. Trio debriefs.

Questioning Dialogue 18 teaches the questioner to probe for similar situations. In the specific strategies offered earlier in Chapter 5 there are frequent steps where the questioner asks a question eliciting a parallel case of some sort in order to seek clarity. One of the most powerful avenues for understanding a complex concept, explanation, or justification involving a document, event, or social issue is the use of parallel cases. This probe is therefore called the parallel case probe.

Though respondents and reactors frequently raise parallel cases themselves, untrained questioners somehow fail to explore them or ask for them. These questioners fail to realize the power of an analogy as an aid in bringing clarity to the topic under study. The respondents and reactors who use parallel cases instinctively know how useful they are in helping their understanding. Since the benefit of using parallel cases is so clear and immediate, questioners do well by learning to elicit them.

Suppose that the respondent says in response to your first question "I believe that we need worldwide nuclear disarmament or else there may be no world." You might well follow with a parallel case probe asking "Is there another issue on which you've taken a similar position?" You might ask "What other issue are you familiar with which also requires a worldwide effort?" Of course, you can phrase the question any way you choose as long as you request the respondent to seek some parallel with the given response on nuclear disarmament. By seeing the issue of nuclear disarmament as analagous to another issue, the respondent receives help in understanding the former. You can, of course, offer an analogy yourself and ask the respondent to accept or approve it.

After the respondent offers a parallel case, you as questioner and other people as reactors can explore the relationship between the issue at hand and the paralle. You can examine the ways in which the two issues are similar and different. You can show how the one sheds light on the other. In exploring the parallels between the two issues the respondent thinks through the issue again with added insight.

Questioning Dialogue 19: Who Supports Probe

1. Trio decides on a common moral or public policy issue.
2. Each person writes at least one starting question calling for an opinion.
3. Trio follows this cycle pattern:
   - **A:** Questions.
   - **B:** Waits to a count of five; C waits also.
   - **B:** Responds with an opinion.
   - **C:** Reacts, if desires.
   - **A:** Questions B or C with a who-supports probe: "Who supports this position?"
   - **B or C:** Responds.
   - **B or C:** Reacts, if desires.
   - **A:** Waits to a count of five and either nods to indicate closure or reacts with a strong and positive rating.
4. Trio rotates and repeats cycle, if possible, built on another starting question.
5. Trio debriefs.

Questioning Dialogue 19 teaches the questioner to focus on the support available for remarks made by the respondent or reactor. Rather than looking ahead by using an implementation or consequences probe, and rather than looking behind by using a how-arrived or why probe, the questioner asks about the acceptability of the remarks by asking who supports those remarks. Hence, this probe is called the who-supports probe.

Suppose your first question is "Do you approve of drafting women as well as men into the army?" Suppose further that the respondent says "No, I don't." You might follow with a who-supports probe, asking "Who supports the opinion you've expressed?" The respondent must then focus on bringing support to the position by naming people or organizations who agree with the position taken. The respondent might say "I heard that even the generals in the U.S. Army claim that women cannot serve as front line soldiers today." In this way the respondent lends weight to the position taken.

After the respondent cites support for the position taken, you as questioner and other people as reactors can explore that support. Is there any real support? Is the support authoritative? Is the support adequate? Does the support convince other people to accept the point of view expressed? In examining the support avialable for the position, the respondent thinks through the issue again. If outside support is lacking or inadequate, the respondent must surely support the position with good personal reasons.

Questioning Dialogue 20: How-Know Probe

1.   Trio decides on an empirical topic such as a natural event, social event, or condition of the universe.
2.   Each person writes at least two starting questions, each calling for a fact about the topic.
3.   Trio follows this cycle pattern:
     A: Questions (using the first starting question.)
     B: Waits to a count of five; C waits also.
     B: Responds with a fact and may give an explanation, if desires.
     C: Reacts, if desires.
     A: Questions B or C with a how-know probe "How do you know that?"

B or C: Responds.
B or C: Reacts.
   A: Waits to a count of five and either nods to indicate closure or reacts with a strong and positive rating.
4. Trio rotates and repeats cycle using second starting question.
5. Trio debriefs.

Questioning Dialogue 20 teaches the questioner to focus on how people know what they know. (The word "know" entails the claim that the statement is true. If I say "I know that the moon rotates around the Earth," I am claiming that this statement about the moon is true.) Hence, this probe is called the how-know probe.

This how-know probe is similar to the who-supports probe but differs from it by being broader. Suppose that for your first question you ask "What is the average winter temperature in Miami, Florida?" Suppose further that the respondent says "It's 75-80° Fahrenheit there." You might follow with a how-know probe asking "How do you know that?" The respondent might reply "I read it in a book," or "My father told me—he was there," or "I was there last winter." It is proper to cite one's personal experience as a source of knowledge: It is not necessary to go to an external source as would be necessary with the narrower who-supports probe.

The benefit of this how-know probe stems from asking people to consider how they know what they know. Some people may claim to know facts because "I just know them," or "Someone told me and I can't remember who it was," or "I heard it in a Donald Duck cartoon on television." These claims to knowledge are not considered to be strong claims. People who become sensitive to knowledge claims seek strong claims—those based on authoritative sources and/or personal experience. The benefit is, therefore, the teaching of a critical approach to considering statements made by people personally, in a newspaper, on radio, on television, or through some other communication medium.

Questioning Dialogue 21: Reasons For Probe

1. Trio decides on a common moral or public policy issue for questions.
2. Each person writes at least one starting question calling for an opinion.
3. Trio follows this cycle pattern:
   A: Questions.
   B: Waits to a count of five; C waits also.
   B: Responds with an opinion and some type of justification (explicit or implicit) which gives support to the opinion.
   A: Questions C with a reasons-for probe: "Why do you think B gave the reasons that he/she did?"
   C: Waits and then responds.
   B: Reacts, if desires.
   A: Waits to a count of five and either nods to indicate closure or reacts with a strong and positive rating.
4. Trio rotates and repeats cycle, if possible, built on another starting question.
5. Trio debriefs.

Questioning Dialogue 21 teaches the questioner to shift from the respondent to another person in searching for the reasons lying behind a given response. With this probe the questioner focuses not on the substance of the response but rather on the respondent's reasons for offering such a response. Thus, this probe is called the reasons-for probe.

Suppose that your first question was "Do you support the legalization of smoking marijuana?" Suppose further that the respondent says "I do because it's not harmful like cigarettes." You might follow with a reasons-for probe to *another person*, asking "Why do you think B responded with that reason?" The new respondent, C, must then focus on B's response by giving reasons for B's reason. This new response might be "Pat said that because that's what he's been telling his parents for the past year. He's trying to convince them that marijuana is O.K." Person B might react to C's response by accepting, denying, or modifying it. In any case, you now have much to explore with the respondents.

In the example above, the questioner probes the reasons given. With two reasons-for probe it is also possible to ask why a particular definition, fact, opinion, or comparison was offered. You need not restrict your probe to reasons for reasons. You may probe for reasons for any given response. You might also probe for reasons for responding hesitantly or whatever other tone you detect in the respondent's voice. Suppose that a respondent says in response to your question on marijuana "Well, see the legalization of, you know, it's, I'm not sure but, well, see, I guess I favor it." You might follow with a reasons for probe "Why do you think B responded so hesitantly and cautiously?" Thus, with this reasons-for probe, you can explore tone as well as content, or whatever other aspect of the response you choose to discuss.

Questioning Dialogue 22:
Dealing with Irrelevant Remarks

1. Trio decides on a common topic for questions.
2. Each person writes at least two questions.
3. Trio follows this cycle pattern:
    A: Questions.
    B: Waits to a count of five; C waits also.
    B: Responds.
    C: Reacts with an (apparent) irrelevant statement.
    A: Questions C, "How is that related to what we're talking about, C?" or "Would you explain how what you're saying is connected to the topic, please?" or any equivalent question.
    C: Responds.
    B: Reacts, if desires.

A: Waits to a count of five and either nods to indicate closure or reacts with a strong and positive rating related to the effort toward clarification.
4.   Trio rotates and repeats cycle.
5.   Trio debriefs.

Questioning Dialogue 22 teaches the questioner a positive way to deal with irrelevant or apparently irrelevant remarks. During a questioning strategy it sometimes occurs that a person, either in responding or reacting, makes a remark which is off-target or seemingly comes out of the blue. Such a remark may catch the questioner off guard. The questioner may be unable to incorporate the remark into the flow of the discourse. The temptation exists to deal with the remark and the speaker in a negative way. This exercise teaches the questioner a technique for dealing with this situation in a constructive way.

Suppose that your first question is on the topic of weather and the respondent says "It's not only the temperature that counts but also the humidity." Suppose further that person C reacts by saying "My grandparents moved to Arizona." Rather than chastise C for saying something which appears irrelevant, it is better for you to ask about the relevancy with the belief that some connection exists in C's head. Therefore you ask "How is your grandparents' moving to Arizona connected to temperature and humidity?" The response, which erases the apparent irrelevancy, might well be "Well, see, the doctor told them to move to a place where it's warm. And since my grandma needed a dry place 'cause she has arthritis, they moved to Arizona rather than Miami where it's wet."

The point here is that people say things which may appear irrelevant. Sometimes the statements are indeed irrelevant. Most of the time there is a definite connection but it is not clear because the speaker is speaking elliptically. That is, the speaker omits part of what's in his/her mind and therefore we don't see the relevancy of the statement. By using the technique of eliciting the relevancy, the questioner helps the speaker clarify statements and has the opportunity to react positively rather than negatively.

Questioning Dialogue 23:
Avoiding Yes-But Reactions

1. Trio decides on a common topic for questions.
2. Each person writes at least two questions calling for a fact or explanation in the empirical mode.
3. Trio follows this cycle pattern:
   - **A:** Questions.
   - **B:** Waits to a count of five; C waits also.
   - **B:** Responds* with an incorrect, partially incorrect, or incomplete remark.
   - **A:** Waits to a count of five and then makes an appropriate move, selecting one from the examples which follow or creating one that is clear and straightforward.
   - **B:** Responds or reacts.
   - **A:** Waits to a count of five and either nods to indicate closure or reacts with a strong and positive rating related to B's second remark or future effort.
4. Trio rotates and repeats cycle.
5. Trio debriefs.

*B may even choose not to respond at all.

Questioning Dialogue 23 teaches you to avoid a common reaction to incorrect, partially correct, or incomplete (inadequate) responses to questions. This reaction is "Yes, but . . ." Questioners often react with "Yes, but" thinking that they are reacting positively to the respondent's remark because they use the word "yes." The expression "Yes, but," however, remains negative and serves a negative function. Its negative characteristic stems in large measure from the fact that the expression is deceptive. Most questioners don't even realize that they have reacted negatively.

Suppose that your question was "Why did it rain yesterday?" The respondent says "Because the air mass coming down from Canada was warm and high pressured." You know that the Canadian air mass was cold, and according to the meteorologist you heard on television the rain was caused by a wet northern-bound wind from the Gulf of Mexico. Rather than react with "Yes, but I heard that it wasn't a Canadian air mass which caused the rain," you can make one of several moves which promote a clearer and more straightforward atmosphere. Among other things, you can:

1. Wait to a count of five with the expectation that another person will volunteer a correction.
2. Rephrase the question in a way that is more likely to elicit the correct response.
3. Ask "Who told you that it was a Canadian air mass?"
4. Ask "How do you know this?"
5. Ask "Is there anyone who wants to comment on B's response?"
6. Say "According to the meteorologist I heard on TV, the cause was a wet wind up from the Gulf of Mexico."
7. Say "That's incorrect." Then continue with another move.
8. Say "B, that's your question. I won't ask anyone else to deal with yesterday's rain. When you have further information on it, you can tell us. If you need help, please call on me." Then proceed with other questions or statements to allow B time to respond correctly.
9. Begin to reteach the patterns and causes of weather conditions in your area via a short presentation at the chalkboard and weather map.
10. Consider B's response as the response to a different question, like "Why does it usually rain in our area?" Then begin question shifting by requesting weather data: "From which direction does a Canadian air mass come?" Then continue to ask other questions to the respondent and other people so as to review, in effect, the facts of yesterday's weather conditions.

The above ten options, I believe, result in a clearer and more straightforward atmosphere than the "Yes, but" reaction. Some people may disagree with some of the options offered. For this reason Questioning Dialogue 23 may well be the most difficult and controversial dialogue of all. Each of the ten options does have its disadvantages and limitations. For this reason, there are only three options worth considering.

There is a potential danger in requesting a second re- spondent to correct the first one. A negative hidden message might be transmitted. ("See? This person knows the answer and is smarter than you. You are inadequate.") Much depends on the way you request help from another respondent. If you ask for someone else to respond, you can soften the request so as to avoid the negative nonverbal message by adding some- thing like "B needs some help here; B has the weather map turned around." You must be careful that you do not embar- rass, humiliate, or poke fun at the first respondent. If the re- quest is done right, the respondent will accept help from someone else in a positive way.

Similarly, you must be careful how you ask the question "How do you know this?" or "Who told you this?" Such a ques- tion, used only after incorrect or incomplete responses, is a threat and challenge to the respondent as well as being a dead giveaway that the response is not acceptable. Such use of this probe (see Questioning Dialogue 20) or any other probe is a violation of the intentions of this entire book's approach to questioning. If, however, you regularly use this how-know probe with all types of responses and reactions, then you eliminate or at least minimize any threat to the respondent.

The eighth option of assigning the respondent the task of doing further work and then reporting to the group stems from the work of Morine and Morine.[4] It is particularly good to use when the intended respondent makes no statement at all. This technique conveys the implicit message, according to Morine and Morine, "You have given an incorrect answer but if I give you enough time, I'm confident you can get the correct answer."[5] This message is important in your effort to turn a

---

[4]Harold Morine and Greta Morine, *Discovery: A Challenge to Teachers* (Englewood Cliffs, N.J.: Prentice-Hall, Inc., 1973), p. 191.
[5]Ibid., p. 193.

situation of failure into one of future success. Of course, you cannot guarantee success; you can only strive to increase the potential for success by creating the opportunity and atmosphere which fosters continued participation by the respondent. For this reason this option may be the best one after waiting five seconds.

Questioning Dialogue 24:
Restating-Crystallizing

1. Trio decides on a common topic for questions.
2. Each person writes at least two questions each calling for a lengthy response.
3. Trio follows this cycle pattern:
   - **A:** Questions.
   - **B:** Waits to a count of five; C waits also.
   - **B:** Responds with a lengthy response—it may even be somewhat confused.
   - **C:** Reacts, if desires.
   - **A:** Questions "Are you saying that . . .?" or an equivalent question which asks B and/or C to respond to A's restatement.
   - **B and/or C:** Responds.
   - **B and/or C:** Reacts, if desires.
   - **A:** Waits to a count of five and nods to indicate closure or reacts with a strong and positive rating.
4. Trio rotates and repeats cycle.
5. Trio debriefs.

Questioning Dialogue 24 teaches you to listen carefully to responses and reactions so that you can check on the essence of statements made. The purpose of your restatement is to capture in capsule form the essence of the remarks and ask if the speakers accept your crystallization. You are not trying to restate verbatim what was said, but you are trying to crystallize in succinct form what the speakers meant.

Suppose that your question was "In your opinion, what was Kennedy's view on Cuba in the early 1960s?" Suppose the respondent says "I feel that he was afraid that Russia would take over Cuba—sort of swallow them up and be closer to the U.S." You might then ask in a restating-crystallizing way "Are you saying that Kennedy feared that Cuba might become Russia's launching pad against the U.S.?" The respondent may respond to this question either yes or no and then embellish upon it with that focus in mind.

You may use the opening phrase "Are you saying that . . ." or any other equivalent such as "As I hear you, you seem to be saying that . . ." and "Do I hear you correctly that . . ." You may also use a reaction and then a question to restate-crystallize if that is easier or preferable. You might in the example above say "It appears to me that you're saying Kennedy feared that Cuba might become Russia's launching pad against the U.S. Is that right?" Whichever you choose, the key to remember is that you are crystallizing what the speakers say. You are focusing on the *content* of the speakers' remarks, seeking to understand and focus them in a capsule form which may be slightly different from what the speakers said.

The purpose of such a crystallizing question is to help the speakers, respondents, and/or reactors to focus their remarks. Sometimes speakers ramble on during a situation and appear unable to see the point they are making. As an alert and trained questioner, you can help them, the other listeners, and yourself. With a clear focus in mind you all can proceed to deal with further points on the topic.

There is also the implicit positive message "I am listening carefully to what you are saying. I believe this is what you are saying. Tell me if I understand you correctly." This is a message which speakers can interpret positively and use as reinforcement. You value their contribution as shown by the attention you pay to their remarks. You must be careful, however, not to overuse this technique lest the speakers feel that all you do is restate-crystallize their remarks.

Questioning Dialogue 25:
Checking Perception of Feelings

1. Trio decides on a common topic for questions.
2. Each person writes at least two questions each calling for a lengthy and/or emotional response.
3. Trio follows this cycle pattern:

    A: Questions.

    B: Waits to a count of five; C waits also.

    B: Responds in an emotional tone without explicitly stating what the emotion is.

    C: Reacts, if desires.

    A: Questions "Am I correct in feeling that you are angry (proud, happy, sad, embarrassed, peeved)?" or an equivalent question which asks B and/or C to respond to a perception regarding their statements.

B and/or C: Responds.

B and/or C: Reacts, if desires.

    A: Waits to a count of five and nods to indicate closure or reacts with a strong and positive rating.

4. Trio rotates and repeats cycle.
5. Trio debriefs.

Questioning dialogue 25 teaches you as questioner to listen carefully to responses and reactions so that you can check on the emotional feeling behind the statements made. (This dialogue is similar to the preceding one.) In the preceding exercise you checked on the content message of the speakers' statements. With this dialogue you check on the speakers' feelings implicit in their statements.

Suppose that your first question was "In your opinion what was Kennedy's view on Cuba in the early 1960s?" Suppose further that the respondent says "Kennedy was afraid of the Russians who were very friendly with the Cubans then. Had Kennedy not stopped them, well we'd have been in trouble. I saw a great movie on Kennedy's decision—tense and dramatic. He was some sharp President." You might then ask in a perception-checking way "Am I correct in feeling that you are satisfied with the outcome and that you are proud of his actions?" The respondent can then respond yes or no, accepting or rejecting your perception of his/her feelings as satisfied and proud. The respondent may go on to elaborate on those feelings with the knowledge that the focus is at least temporarily on the feelings implicit in the remarks rather than the content of those remarks.

Sometimes you may find it easier to check perceptions by combining your question with a reaction. In the example above you might first react by saying "It seems to me that you're satisfied with the outcome and that you're proud of his actions." Then follow with the question "Is that so?" Either procedure leads to perception checking and is acceptable as long as you focus on the respondent's feelings as manifested in the remark made.

The purpose of perception checking is to focus attention on the implied feelings which may be the real message behind the response. Sometimes a respondent tries to curb or cover feelings, thinking that you will not permit them to enter into consideration. Sometimes a respondent is simply too shy or too stubborn to use emotional tags explicitly and sends only implied messages. Sometimes respondents are simply unaware of their feelings on a given topic. Whatever the case, you should consider the feelings manifested as a critical item in the issue. If so, the technique of perception checking and focusing allows you a way of asking the respondent or reactor about feelings. You must be careful, however (as with restating-crystallizing), not to overwork this technique.

SEVEN

TEACHING STRATEGIES, GOALS, AND QUESTIONS

In recent years the term 'teaching strategy' has become quite popular in education. Perhaps it doesn't rank with other terms such as "structure of the disciplines," "whole child," "back to basics," "team teaching," "open classroom," and "individualized instruction." Yet the concern for teaching strategies has existed for years at a lower level of interest and will no doubt persist in the future when other terms will have been forgotten. In any case, the rise of the recent interest in strategies of teaching came at a time in the 1960s when there was renewed investigation into both curriculum and actual classroom teaching. The purpose of teaching strategies is to help teachers in achieving their goals by formulating appropriate guidelines for and sequences of actions to take during the complex interaction of teaching.

This chapter looks at teaching strategies and then teaching goals as a way of setting a framework within which questions are asked. At the same time, it further explores the role of questions in relation to teaching strategies and goals.

TEACHING STRATEGIES[1]

Roots

The current rise in interest in teaching strategies stems from two movements that gained popularity in the 1960s. The first, the curriculum reform movement, is commonly associated with Bruner and his followers.[2] Educators sought new ways to revitalize teaching in the schools. They were aware that there was more than one way to teach. The educational literature of the 1920s, 1930s, and 1940s had called on teachers to shift their emphasis and approach. Yet one method still predominated across the country. With the design of new curricular projects from nursery school through graduate and professional school came the pressing need for a variety of teaching approaches. The conception of a particular project demanded a particular teaching strategy or strategies. Teachers could not implement the new curriculums unless they adopted teaching approaches in harmony with the projects.

The second movement, the study of verbal interaction in the classroom, is commonly associated with Flanders, Smith, Bellack, Gallagher, Aschner, and Hughes, among others.[3] This movement arose as a result of the desire by educators to know more about what teachers actually do in the classroom rather than what they should do. Related to this study of verbal interaction were the concurrent movements in (1) philosophy, which set out to describe the uses of ordinary language, and (2) educational research, which set out to delineate at least the groundwork for a theory of teaching.[4] These

---

[1]This section, with some modification, originally appeared in my article, "Teaching Strategies for Pluralistic Teaching," *Issues in Secondary Education*, Seventy-fifth Yearbook, Part II of the National Society for the Study of Education (Chicago: National Society for the Study of Education, 1976), pp. 240-68.

[2]Jerome S. Bruner, *The Process of Education* (Cambridge: Harvard University Press, 1960); idem, *On Knowing* (Cambridge: Harvard University Press, 1962).

[3]Ronald T. Hyman, ed., *Teaching: Vantage Points for Study*, 2nd ed. (Philadelphia: J.B. Lippincott Company, 1974).

[4]Ronald T. Hyman, ed., *Contemporary Thought on Teaching* (Englewood Cliffs, N.J.: Prentice-Hall, Inc., 1971), Parts I and II.

educators realized from their descriptions of the verbal interaction in classrooms that a common and uniform approach to teaching persisted despite the enthusiastic requests for and the acceptances of alternative strategies. They further recognized the need to specify clearly the teaching strategies that could serve as alternatives to the existing patterns of classroom interaction.

It is significant that many of the educators who subsequently delved into the development and popularization of alternative teaching strategies were precisely those who were closely associated with one of the two foundation movements mentioned above. For example, Taba based her prescriptive strategies on her descriptive studies of thought processes in the classroom.[5] These strategists' efforts, therefore, are an outgrowth of previous work rather than a superimposed trend or an opposite trend appearing out of context and springing full grown from the heads of educational faddists.

Types of Teaching Strategies and Their Rationales

There are three main types of teaching strategies, classified and named according to the essential activity of the teacher: exemplifying, enabling, and presenting. Each type has its distinctive characteristics, rationale, advantages, and disadvantages. Let us examine these three strategies closely.

The three names for the strategies are deliberately stipulated. First, the name of each strategy offers a capsuled idea of the teacher's intent and activity when utilizing that particular strategy. Second, the names are couched in plain and clear English in order to facilitate comprehension and to avoid confusion and vagueness. Third, the names are new so as to eliminate associations teachers may have with previous labels for strategies that are identified with a particular group of people, curriculum project, or philosophy.

[5]Hilda Taba and Freeman F. Elzey, "Teaching Strategies and Thought Processes," in *Teaching: Vantage Points for Study*, pp. 483-500.

Several more common labels are therefore missing. Take the case of "heuristics," a word of Greek derivation, which was a popular term in the 1960s. Most classroom teachers did not and still do not understand that word. What is worse, the term "heuristics" misleads many teachers, for it often appears as a synonym for "discovery" teaching. But discovery is generally designated as the goal of the student, not the teacher, and hence teachers do not receive help and clues about what the teacher should do when following the exhortation that they should engage in heuristics or discovery teaching. Thus, the terms "heuristics" and "discovery," as well as the terms "didactics," "guidance," "modeling," and "expository" are absent from the descriptions of strategies found in this book.

The Presenting Strategy

At this time the strategy best known in its various forms is the presenting strategy. Most teachers consciously use the presenting strategy more than enabling and exemplifying. The lecture and recitation belong to this type of strategy, in which the teachers put forth the information to be received and learned by the students. Usually the teachers do this orally; occasionally they do so in writing. Teachers can be live persons or a substitute in the form of a textbook, film, recording, or computerized program. The students receive and process the information presented in order to understand the message transmitted to them. Sometimes the message is a general idea or belief. At other times the message sent by the teacher is a group of specific information units. The students then either particularize the general message or generalize from the specifics. They may do so through the aid of some checkup questions prepared by the teachers, but they do so mainly through their own efforts. The teachers often particularize or generalize for the students. The students then relate their new learning to their own lives and act upon it in the future.

The presenting strategy is based on the following ideas:

1. The teacher knows what information the student needs to know.
2. The teacher is personally familiar with the needed information.
3. The teacher can effectively transmit the message containing the information to the student.
4. The student can cope with the highly symbolic nature of this strategy (symbolic in that the teacher's message comes mostly through oral channels).
5. The student can particularize and generalize from transmitted messages, relate the teacher's messages to life outside the classroom, and act on symbolically derived learning.

In the presenting strategy the teachers are the more active participants physically, cognitively, and emotionally. They select the information, organize it, present it, re-present it in an effort to be clear and comprehensible, and question the student in order to be sure that the students are understanding. The teachers are diagnosticians, selectors, organizers, synthesizers, presenters, questioners, and examiners. The students are mainly receivers and relaters in the classroom. The students are usually expected to act on their new learning out of class rather than in class or in connection with the presentation. The physical, cognitive, and emotional load of the students is not nearly as great as that of the teacher.

The greatest single advantage of presenting is its generational efficiency. Through this strategy each generation of students can benefit easily from its predecessors. Were it not for our ability to learn through symbolic crystallization and transmission of information, each generation would be forced to rediscover how to make a fire, how to make a wheel, how to write, how to calculate, how to cure diseases, how to build bridges, how to make telephones, and so forth. The teacher who presents can teach about many topics in a short period of time.

Other advantages of the presenting strategy are related to its generational efficiency. Because they are not significantly taxed physically, cognitively, or emotionally, students can devote themselves to several teachers and their messages simultaneously. The low expenditure of energy allows the students to study longer and hence receive more messages. The presenting strategy also suits many students who do not feel ready to study on their own, who do not have the resources available to do so, or who prefer to listen to an experienced, knowledgeable person.

The disadvantages of presenting are equally apparent. Many students simply do not have the cognitive ability to cope with the symbolic nature of the transmitted messages. Their ability to understand, relate, and then apply the messages is limited. Such students learn little through this strategy. Furthermore, since most of the decisions and tasks dealing with the information come from the teacher, the student may not even be interested enough to exert the necessary effort to receive, perceive, relate, and apply the message. The message may not be meaningful to the students because they are not sufficiently involved with it. When meaningfulness and interest are lacking, the students often do not exert the cognitive attention and energy needed to perceive, to particularize, to generalize, to relate, and to apply the message. If forced to do these tasks by teachers through extrinsic rewards, threats, tests, or checkup questions, students may become hostile. On the other hand, teachers fear that without such extrinsic and coercive techniques students may quickly forget what they have learned. Such means and such results have their own well-known limitations and need no further comment here.

Though it may be possible to employ the presenting strategy without asking any questions—the proverbial professors who enter the lecture hall, open their notes, lecture, close their notes, and exit without speaking or hearing another word—in practice, questions take on a crucial role in presenting.

Consider first the lecture, the quintessential method used in the presenting strategy. Via questions during and after the teacher has transmitted the ideas to the students, students attempt to clarify matters. They seek elucidation and explication. The questions serve the teacher as sign posts regarding the level and areas of understanding and misunderstanding.

With a quick diagnosis the teacher can and does move to further the students' understanding. The teacher, too, asks questions during and after a lecture to get feedback from the students so as to know what to emphasize and what to modify. The teacher often solicits questions from the students with "Do you have any questions now?" This not-so-subtle solicitation acknowledges that the teacher needs questions for guidance and diagnosis just as the students need questions for clarification when the lecture method is used.

Other methods such as recitation and programmed instruction (in book form or computer assisted form) rely even more heavily on questions. In the recitation the teacher's questions serve as the elicitor of the information to be made public for all students to hear and learn. After the student recites the information—note that the word's root is "re-cite," to cite again from the textbook, film, teacher's lecture, or some other source—the teacher often adds further information before asking another question. In this way the questions indicate which information the students are to present to each other for learning. In programmed instruction the questions serve as a way of getting feedback on the student's understanding so as to branch into the appropriate sections of the program that will lead to mastery of the material presented.

The Enabling Strategy

The second type of strategy is enabling. The enabling strategy is not widely used in schools even though recent educational literature is replete with urgings and guidelines for it. The reasons for this situation are several and complex. For one thing, the teacher needs more sophistication, experience, desire, and involvement with students to teach as an enabler. Discussion, brainstorming, laboratory activities, and problem-solving projects belong to the enabling strategy.

In the enabling strategy the students engage in some activity, most often under the supervision of the teacher. Generally and preferably the activity concerns a problem to be solved. Teachers need not participate in the activity, although they gain by doing so. When teachers do participate with the students, they must continually remember that their task is to "enable" the students, not to solve the problem for them. The teachers must encourage and allow the students to take the lead as the activity progresses. Preferably, teachers and students select the activity together, although this need not be the case.

The activity may not arise from a problem facing the students but rather from interest, curiosity, or as part of an everyday activity. Students may be interested in knowing about the moon as it orbits the earth. They begin to read about previous investigations, observe the moon with a telescope, read the accounts of the astronauts, perhaps even interview or correspond with the astronauts, and calculate further movements of the moon and their effect on the earth. The teacher and students recount or report on the essential particulars of the subject in order to be fully aware of them and to understand them. The students then generalize from the specifics to some abstract idea on their own. The students then apply the generalization they have learned to their future lives in and out of the classroom.

If the activity arises from a problem to be solved, then the teacher and students clearly formulate what the problem is through definition and analysis. They offer a hypothesis that serves as the basis for the subsequent collection of relevant data. They analyze and try to explain the data. They test the hypothesis to see if it indeed solves the problem. If they do not accept the hypothesis, they formulate another hypothesis. If need be, they might even reformulate the problem situation so as to clarify it. Once a tested hypothesis is accepted, they apply what they have learned to their lives in and out of the classroom.

The teacher's role in the enabling strategy is obviously not to perform the cognitive tasks for the students. Rather it is to enable the students to generalize from the particulars of the activity, to formulate and test hypotheses. The teacher enables the students by directing them in the processes involved in learning from their own activities. The teacher enables them to interpret their own experiences through helpful, appropriate questions and suggestions. Since the intent is to enable, the teacher does not ask questions in a quizzing tone but in a helping tone. The teacher steps in, makes suggestions, and asks questions only when it is necessary to enable the students to proceed on their own.

The enabling strategy is based on the following ideas:

1. Students gain skills, knowledge, and beliefs meaningfully through activities they are involved in themselves.
2. Students will probably act on generalizations and test hypotheses with which they have been actively concerned themselves.
3. There is intrinsic motivation to learn and remember what is learned when activity arises out of interest, curiosity, or a problem.
4. Teachers can enable students to learn to think analytically and creatively by suggesting, prodding, challenging, and leading, since teachers cannot meaningfully abstract an idea for the student or apply an idea to the students' lives.
5. Students perform cognitive tasks well and with significance when they are physically, emotionally, and cognitively involved in the activity.

In the enabling strategy, teachers are not necessarily as physically active as the students. Teachers may participate with the student in the activity although this is not essential. It may be pedagogically advisable, however, for the teacher to participate so as to establish a good relationship with the students, to be aware of the particulars of the activity from which the students will generalize, and to be aware of the ramifications of the problem situation as well as the hypotheses formulated. If the problem faces both the teacher and the students, then of course the teacher must participate.

The advantages of the enabling strategy are several. First, students learn willingly, enthusiastically, and meaningfully when they have an active, relevant stake in the teaching situation. The students learn generalizations and solutions to problems because they have been involved integrally. Second, in a problem situation the solving of a pertinent problem is itself a reward. It removes feelings of perplexity, distress, and obstruction, and it brings a sense of success and satisfaction. Third, the students learn with practice how to benefit from an activity or problem situation because they have learned how to proceed to generalizations and acceptable solutions. Fourth, there is, therefore, little or no need for extrinsic reward because of the overall intrinsic reward of becoming an able person. Ability, as a result of enabling, is its own reward.

The disadvantages of the enabling strategy center on the degree of sophistication required of the teacher. Teachers need to understand the processes of generalizing and problem solving as well as the developmental status of the students relative to these processes. They need to be insightful so that the activities of the students are pertinent and have potential for meaningfulness. They must be able to restrain themselves from doing the tasks of the students when they see that they (teachers) can do the tasks better and faster themselves. Teachers must be able to allow students to fail in generalizing or solving a problem, and must encourage them to learn from the experience as the students try again with additional help. In short, teachers must constantly keep in mind that their task is to enable the students to learn.

Because the enabling strategy relies on activity that is meaningful, and because it is not possible for the teacher to know in advance what all the particulars of that activity will be, it is difficult to plan in great detail. In the short run this strategy is time consuming since it requires the development of activities and problems to create a solid foundation upon which to build. It takes time to generate many potentially fruitful particulars and to formulate hypotheses. Since the teacher must follow the flow of the activities that are meaningful, devote considerable time to the activities and their outgrowths, and schedule loosely rather than follow a tight plan, it is virtually impossible in most teaching situations to "cover" a given area of study exhaustively and systematically. Furthermore, since the aim is to enable the students to think critically, analytically, and creatively, it is difficult for most teachers to test and assess the learning of the students.

The key to the enabling strategy is questioning. The enabling strategy absolutely requires questions, from the teacher or the students. Consider the discussion method: Unless a question is posed, there is nothing to discuss. There need not be an outpouring of questions, but there must be a critical few that cause the respondents to react with each other. If there are too many questions and not enough responses and reactions, there is no discussion at all. Questions raise the issue and then serve to direct which subparts of the issue the teacher and students will pursue in depth.

The Exemplifying Strategy

The third strategy, exemplifying, is the least used by teachers. Teachers do not often consciously and deliberately exemplify what they speak about so that the students will learn through the teacher's example. Teachers may at times exemplify certain skills, such as how to spell correctly, and certain moral beliefs, such as being honest. But they do not exemplify many other important skills and beliefs. In general, teachers do not strategically engage in exemplary action so that their students can observe and learn from the example.

This is not to claim that teachers never exemplify particular behaviors. In whatever teachers do they are exemplifying something to their students. Much of what teachers exemplify, however, is unintentional and nonstrategic. Worse yet, much is inconsistent or dissonant with the explicit aims and verbal statements of the teachers. This unintentional exemplification is part of the hidden agenda or unstudied curriculum in schools. The hidden agenda is impressive in its extent and the unstudied curriculum is often the one that students learn, remember, and act upon in the present and future.

The exemplifying strategy is particularly suited to the teaching of skills, processes, and values. With this strategy the teacher can show the student how to hammer, how to repair a flat tire, how to establish testable hypotheses, how to conduct research, how to arrange data so as to make generalizations, how an honest person acts, how a person respects other individuals, and how a person acts fairly. By exemplifying, the teacher allows the students to see for themselves the consequences of all these actions as well as how to perform them.

This strategy is also suited to teaching facts and generalizations. Obviously, teachers cannot exemplify a fact or explanation or principle in the same way they can exemplify a skill or manifest a value. But teachers can demonstrate and thereby have their actions serve as a particular instance of a general case for the students to witness. Teachers use the exemplifying strategy when they deliberately demonstrate a fact or generalization.

In the exemplifying strategy teachers set up or build upon situations, appropriate in time and place, that have the potential for them to exemplify what they want the students to learn. They arrange the necessary materials. They clarify for themselves the concepts, skills, processes, and beliefs involved in the forthcoming activity as best they can foresee them. Then, after they have thought out what they will do, the teachers engage in the activity publicly. The students may participate with the teachers if the activity is a joint one or one that focuses on a common concern. The teachers exemplify what they want the students to learn in their actions and the students watch them. Sometimes, in the case of creative work such as poetry or painting, the students may see only the finished piece without seeing the teachers actually handle the pencils and brushes. (It is preferable that the students see the whole process.) Teachers may or may not comment on the activity as they go along. The students relate what they see and learn to their own lives and act on what they have learned in similar situations in the future.

The exemplifying strategy is based on the following ideas:

1. Students learn from watching a model and imitating it.
2. Students learn from concrete and meaningful examples in the classroom, just as they have done from the first minutes of their lives.
3. The teacher does not necessarily verbalize or needs only minimal verbalization as an accompaniment to strategic exemplification.
4. It is only natural and sensible for teachers to exemplify a harmony among objectives, verbal action, and nonverbal action since the students learn from them all.
5. Many students respond better to the primarily nonverbal model exemplified by what teachers do than to the verbal language spoken by the teachers.[6]

Exemplifying is primarily a nonverbal mode of teaching. Teachers may, if they choose, comment verbally on what they are doing as a means of reinforcing their points or assuring themselves that they are communicating their messages to the students. This is what Socrates did with Meno, as mentioned earlier. Even if we argue that at some point teachers must necessarily comment on their actions, the nonverbal aspect is still the essential one.

The advantages of the exemplifying strategy relate to this nonverbal element. First, many students (especially the young and the inexperienced ones, but older people too) can learn from a nonverbal message but have difficulty with a verbal, symbolic one. In teaching generalized conservation to young students researchers found that only the exemplifying procedures, and not conventional or verbal explanation, were effective with disadvantaged Mexican-Americans.[7] Second, the exemplifying strategy continues a communication form that is prominent in life outside the classroom. Much of what

[6]For the value of shared experiences see the last part of the essay by R.S. Peters, "Education as Initiation," in *Philosophical Analysis and Education*, ed. Reginald D. Archambault (New York: The Humanities Press, 1965), pp. 87-111.

[7]Barry J. Zimmerman and F. Susan Ghozeil, "Modeling as a Teaching Technique," *Elementary School Journal*, 74 (April 1974), 440-46.

people learn is learned by imitating the nonverbal examples they see about them. We learn how to eat, talk, and walk by imitating the deliberate and nondeliberate examples of other people. To learn from examples is a natural way of life for people, including students. These two advantages are put succinctly in an old limerick:

> *There once was a person named Beecher*
> *Successful, effective, great teacher.*
> *"I'll tell you the key:*
> *What I teach them is ME,*
> *I serve as a model, not preacher."**

Third, via the exemplifying strategy teachers have an effective means of concretizing the abstract values, principles, and processes they wish to teach. Teachers are wary of verbalizing abstract points in simple terms, and rightfully so, since many times their efforts only result in further symbolic complexity. The exemplifying strategy offers a way of avoiding this trouble.

Fourth, the exemplifying strategy elicits from students whatever action they are capable of performing but for some reason are not doing at the time. When teachers exemplify an activity they encourage students to draw on their repertoire of abilities to perform new actions. The new actions are then more likely to occur than before.[8]

Fifth, the exemplifying strategy, because it continues a natural and deep-seated way of learning, forms a bridge between school and society. This bridge brings meaning to the teaching situation as it relates that situation to other life activities. It shows that the teacher is a real person engaged in real activities.

Sixth, the use of the exemplifying strategy serves to motivate the teachers. No matter which strategy the teachers

[8]Ibid., 442.

*"Teaching Strategies for Pluralistic Teaching," *Issues in Secondary Education*, Seventy-fifth Yearbook, Part II of the National Society for the Study of Education (Chicago: National Society for the Study of Education, 1976).

use, they benefit when they teach. The acts of preparing, organizing, clarifying, and reclarifying all benefit teachers as well as the students. There is indeed truth to the popular adage that a good way to learn something is to teach it to others. But the exemplifying strategy benefits the teachers more than the presenting and enabling strategies. The teachers get caught up in the situation more easily and quickly when they exemplify. The activity can serve as a springboard for future activity outside of teaching, since the distinction between the teaching activity and other life activity quickly fades away.

The case of Harry Kemelman serves to support this point. Kemelman, a teacher of English at Boston State College, was teaching a class in advanced composition and trying to show his students "that words do not exist *in vacuo* but have meanings that can transcend their usual connotations, that even short combinations can permit a wide variety of interpretations." Kemelman got caught up in his attempt at making inferences and projections and then finally sat down himself to write a story based on his own thinking. The result was a short detective story featuring Nicholas Welt, a professor who solved problems by pure logic. Out of the Nicky Welt series of stories, Kemelman achieved public acclaim with his detective novels, beginning with *Friday the Rabbi Slept Late*, winner of the Mystery Writers of America "Edgar" for the best first mystery novel of the year. Kemelman has commented that "Rabbi David Small can be said to be the son of Professor Nicholas Welt" who "was born in the classroom."[9]

The disadvantages of the exemplifying strategy begin with the difficulty of setting up teaching situations where teachers can smoothly and comfortably exemplify the skills, values, and principles they wish their students to learn. If the situation appears odd, the effect of this strategy will decrease. Second, once they have established appropriate teaching situ-

---

[9]Harry Kemelman, *The Nine Mile Walk: The Nicky Welt Stories* (New York: G.P. Putnam's Sons, 1967), pp. 9-12.

ations, it is hard for teachers to determine to what extent they are communicating their messages to their students. Teachers may think they are exemplifying a skill or value to the students yet the students may not be perceiving the intended message. If and when teachers check with students, they may spoil the smooth flow of nonverbal activity, and remove the desired subtlety of the communication.

Third, it is difficult to measure the learning of the students based on the exemplifying strategy. Since any exemplified activity has multiple dimensions that the student can witness and learn, it is difficult to test precisely what and to what degree the student has learned. The testing issue is important to teachers who desire to or are required to test their students.

Fourth, the students may find it difficult to observe the teacher intimately over a sustained period of time, to extract the essential elements of the activity for emphasis and learning, and finally to apply the exemplified, nonverbal message to their own situations. This disadvantage exists today in large measure because under current practices students simply do not have enough classroom experience in learning from the exemplifying strategy.

In the exemplifying strategy the teacher can avoid asking questions. But the teacher cannot prevent questions from the students. Although the exemplifying strategy is basically nonverbal, the student asks questions in order to clarify matters. Students can and do "read" the teacher's nonverbal actions all the time. Nevertheless, nonverbal actions are always subject to personal interpretation. Hence, the students ask questions in an effort to ascertain and clarify. The perceptive teacher welcomes questions, for they serve the purposes of clarification and feedback simultaneously.

Thus, no matter which strategy teachers employ, questions will arise and will be critical. It is true that there may be more questions with the enabling strategy than with the presenting or exemplifying strategies. The lower quantity of questions, however, does not deny the need for questions. Students often leave a lecture where no questions were permitted and feel frustrated. They say "I wish I could have asked a question; I don't understand that one point and the rest hangs on it."

GOALS FOR TEACHING

The three teaching strategies—presenting, enabling, and exemplifying—relate to other aspects of teaching, including a key aspect, goals. Strategies relate to goals and do so in such a way as to give added meaning to both the strategies and the goals.

It is possible to categorize the goals of teaching in several ways. One convenient, understandable, and yet simple way is to consider the twofold nature of goals. First, some goals of teaching are social in nature. With such goals, teachers focus on the social, political, and economic elements of life. The teacher aims to help the students understand life and become participating members of society.

School teachers do not teach students to live a totally solitary life. Teachers recognize that students will find themselves participating as members of small groups and large groups at different times. Accordingly, teachers conduct their activities with their students in varying group sizes so as to provide conccrete experiences on which to build. Teachers do and should comment on appropriate behavior in a small group and large group as a way of further achieving the social goals of teaching. In line with this social nature of goals, teachers teach appropriate skills and processes of group behavior, values, and knowledge.

Second, some goals focus on the individual aspects of life. Here teachers see the students themselves as functioning persons. Teachers aim to help the students to develop in three different but related realms. One realm involves knowledge and thinking (the cognitive realm). Teachers teach their students how to gather information and process information so as to gain knowledge. They help students to perform various cognitive operations such as remembering, generalizing, analyzing, and synthesizing. The aim is to teach the students to think critically and reflectively for themselves as they gather and process information in various ways.

Another realm involves values and emotions (the affective realm). Teachers aim to help the students understand themselves and develop their individual interests and talents. Teachers foster personal growth, which includes the psychological, aesthetic, ethical, and metaphysical dimensions of life. Each student is a unique person experiencing a particular way of life.

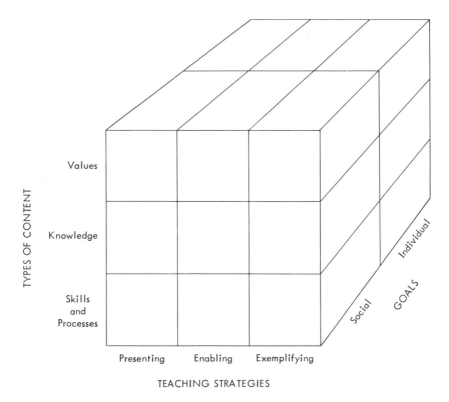

Figure 7-1   The Interrelationships Between Teaching Strategies, Goals, and Types of Content.

The third realm involves the body (the physical or psychomotor realm). Teachers aim to help the student use their bodies to perform many complex actions and skills. Students learn how to coordinate mind with body (particularly hands and legs) to perform the skills people need and desire, such as writing, tying knots, painting, cutting, measuring, swimming, and sawing, etc.

In line with this personal nature of goals, teachers teach appropriate skills and processes of individual behavior, values, and knowledge in the cognitive, affective, and physical realms.

We can show the interrelationships of teaching strategies, goals, and types of content taught with Figure 7-1.

Questions are essential in teaching with regard to both types of goals and all three types of content. Teachers and students ask questions when they are engaged in achieving social goals and individual goals, and they often do not distinguish between these two types of goals in a specific teaching situation. Nor do students—or teachers for that matter—clearly distinguish between the three types of content in a specific teaching situation. The types blend together as the teaching occurs. In summary, teachers and students ask questions as they move along, for questions are essential to their verbal interaction regardless of strategy, goal, or content.

EIGHT

CONCLUSION

This final chapter ties together the many points made in this book. I shall not attempt to offer one universal recipe as the panacea for effective classroom questioning since I believe such a prescription does not and cannot exist due to the complexity of the issue. Just as this book began with a modest approach to questioning, so it will end with the modest hope that those who make a first step towards using a sharpened view on questioning will have the courage, motivation, and success to build upon the points made here.

BRIEF RESTATEMENT OF KEY POINTS

1. Questioning is essential to teaching; both for the teacher and the student.
2. A question can and does serve a plurality of purposes simultaneously.
3. The primary purpose of a question is to spur a person to think and to direct that person to think about a particular topic.
4. There are several ways of categorizing questions. I have used the

concept of thinking processes, compatible with the primary purpose of questions, as the foundation for categorizing questions.

5. The categories for questions in teaching include three main types—definitional, empirical, and evaluative—which can be subdivided into an expanded set of five categories. (See Chapter 2 for these categories.)

6. You can also categorize questions according to production type, information-process activity, and response clue.

7. To provide for a rich variety of perspectives and frameworks, teachers need a plurality of questioning strategies to guide them.

8. The five general strategies for asking questions are mixed, peaks, plateaus, inductive, and deductive.

9. The fifteen specific strategies focus on providing a tool for leading respondents to perform such cognitive tasks as generalizing, explaining, and resolving value conflicts.

10. The twenty-five questioning dialogues provide a means for you to learn such fundamental techniques as waiting, probing, and checking back with another speaker.

11. All the strategies and questioning dialogues are tools for you to use. Modify, amend, improve upon, and increase them. They are dynamic rather than static. They are servants, not masters.

12. In each of the three types of teaching strategies—presenting, enabling, and exemplifying—questions can and do play a significant role.

13. Questions help the teacher achieve the social, individual, and content related goals.

14. Teaching is essentially a verbal activity.

FINAL POINTS

It is not enough for you to read this book. It is not enough to study the category system offered here. It is not enough to read through the five general strategies, the fifteen specific strategies, and the twenty-five questioning dialogues. It is necessary for you to read carefully and then to begin to use these tools—the category system, the general strategies, the specific strategies, and the questioning dialogues. Only by actually implementing the many techniques for improved questioning will you begin to reap the benefit of the seeds planted here. The harvest comes when you have begun to use these techniques—as they are or with some unique modification—in your own teaching.

These techniques for improved questioning are not ends in themselves, just as questioning is not an end in itself. The aim is improved teaching for the social and individual benefit of the students and their supporting society. The aim is to help you teach better so that your students will profit. The purpose is not only to present a book that you can discuss with colleagues and friends, but to offer you some tools for improving your ability to ask questions while you teach so you can meaningfully increase your students' verbal participation when interacting with you.

It is essential for every teacher to keep in mind at all times that the purpose of questioning—and all teacher pedagogical techniques—is the facilitation of student participation in learning the material at hand. As mentioned in the Introduction, language must become a facilitating force rather than an impediment to learning. The way you ask a question, as well as the place that question has in the overall sequence of questions, is an important factor. Moreover, according to Gage, director of the Program on Teaching Effectiveness at Stanford University, you should call on a student by name "*before* asking the question." This technique of preselecting the respondent is a means of providing each student an equal number of opportunities to answer your questions.[1] Since tone is important, you should ask your questions in a way which conveys to the respondent that you are seeking an informative response—that you are encouraging participation, that you are trying to create a nonthreatening situation, that you are seeking to foster thinking which will lead to the achievement of valid educational goals.

It seems obvious that one of the essential ways of

---

[1]N.L. Gage, *The Scientific Basis of the Art of Teaching* (New York: Teachers College Press, 1978) p. 39.

facilitating student participation and learning is the encouragement of student questions. In one study by Blank and Covington, pupils who were given a complete program designed to guide them to ask questions not only learned to ask more questions than the control group but also received higher scores on the test given to both groups. Furthermore, this experimental group received higher ratings in regard to classroom participation in discussions.[2] In another study focusing on student questioning and achievement the data show that the more problem oriented the students' questions, the higher their scores on a problem test.[3]

The Harvard educational philosopher, Schleffler, in his chapter essay entitled "Moral Education and the Democratic Ideal," sees questioning as the key means of becoming critical, of learning to reason and be reasonable.[4] He places great weight on questioning and reasonableness since he sees reasonableness as the connecting link for the moral, scientific, and democratic education of our citizens. Questioning, so to speak, becomes the modern Atlas, supporting the educational heavens on its shoulders and promoting in students the ability to reason, as citizens in a twentieth century democracy must do. Scheffler says:

> In training our students to reason we train them to be critical. We encourage them to ask questions, to look for evidence, to seek and scrutinize alternatives, to be critical of their own ideas as well as others. This educational course precludes taking schooling as an instrument for shaping their minds to a preconceived idea. For if they seek reasons, it is their evaluation of such reasons that will determine what ideas they eventually accept.[5]

[2]Stanley S. Blank and Martin Covington, "Inducing Children to Ask Questions in Solving Problems," *The Journal of Education Research*, 59, no. 1 (September 1965), pp. 21-27.
[3]Susan Lynne Bernstein, "The Effects of Children's Question-Asking Behavior on Problem Solution and Comprehension of Written Material" (abstract of unpublished Doctoral dissertation, Columbia University, 1973).
[4]Israel Scheffler, *Reason and Teaching* (Indianapolis: The Bobbs-Merrill Co., 1973).
[5]Ibid., p. 143.

Perhaps it will be wise for you to teach your students to ask questions by teaching them some of the essentials of the strategies and techniques offered in this book. Their subsequent influence on you as teachers can be significant.[6] It will surely be helpful if you actively solicit student questions and patiently wait for them. One proverbial professor entered the classroom and asked for questions. Hearing none, he left. At the next class session, he again asked for questions from the students regarding the topic at hand. Hearing none, he left again. When finally a student asked him a question at the third session, he introduced his response with "Now we can begin to study." The word "question" comes from the Latin root meaning "to inquire," and so this professor began to interact with his students when they began to inquire.

You can explicitly ask for questions simply by saying "Please ask some questions." Research by Moskal[7] indicates that when teachers ask for questions (for example, "Are there any questions?"), students do indeed ask them. Or you can ask each student to write down one question and then have all the students read their questions one by one. You can so group the students that they ask each other questions within the small groups, dealing with selected aspects of the topic at hand. The main point is that you demonstrate to the students your sincerity and satisfaction when they do ask questions. In this way you reinforce their desires and willingness to ask questions.

It is necessary for you to encourage students to ask questions because the current number and percentage of student questions are low.[8] It is shocking to learn from Dodl that "it is

[6]See the research of Willis D. Copeland, "The Relationship Between Microteaching and Student Teacher Classroom Performance," *The Journal of Educational Research*, 68, no. 8 (April 1975), pp. 289-93; and "Some Factors Related to Student Teacher Classroom Performance Following Microteaching Training," *American Educational Research Journal*, 14, no. 2 (Spring 1977), pp. 147-57.

[7]Krystyna Moskal, "The Effects of Interventions and Personality on Elementary School Teachers' Question-Eliciting Behavior" (Doctoral dissertation, Rutgers University, 1978).

[8]See the review article on questioning by Meredith D. Gall, "The Use of Questions in Teaching," *Review of Educational Research*, 40, no. 5 (December 1970), 707-20.

quite clear that pupil questions arise very infrequently during social studies instructional situations. Of a total of 43,531 behavior incidences recorded during this study, only 728 were pupil questions. For a behavior to occur only 1.67 percent of such a large sample seems to be adequate evidence to support hypotheses which use the absence of pupil questions as their basis."[9] In short, students don't ask many questions despite the cries of some teachers that students are always asking why.

Even if you do succeed in getting your students to ask questions of you and each other, you need to remember that questioning is only one pedagogical technique. Some students may choose to participate in the classroom language game mainly through their reactions to you and other students. The essential point is the *quality* of a student's participation in both content and pedagogical function, and not the *quantity* of questions asked. That is to say, the quality of participation is a combination of content and function. You must take steps to assure that your students do not become full-time astute respondents to you or mere questioners without direction simply to increase the quantity of their questions. Quality participation necessitates a mixture of pedagogical function with substantive focus—asking appropriate questions, responding correctly or validly to queries, reacting pointedly to others' statements, and structuring classroom topics or activities.

In the last analysis, you will teach your students how to participate in teaching by the way you yourself participate. Above all, the message of your teaching is what you do. You are a model whether or not you choose to be one. As stated in Chapter 7

> *"What I teach them is ME,*
> *I serve as a model, not preacher."*

---

[10]Norman R. Dodl, "Questioning Behavior of Elementary Classroom Groups," *California Journal of Instructional Improvement*, 9, no. 3 (October 1966), 167–79.

By planning carefully, by questioning strategically, and by interacting with your students meaningfully as they talk with you, you have the opportunity to exemplify how to succeed in playing the teaching language game.

Surely the single best educational audio-visual teaching aid is an alert, attentive, sensitive, sophisticated teacher. With sincerity of purpose, excellent practice, and determination you can become such a teacher. The question is, "Do you care enough about your teaching?"

Index